ACCOUNTING AND FINANCIAL REPORTING FOR GOVERNMENTAL AND NONPROFIT ORGANIZATIONS

BASIC CONCEPTS

ACCOUNTING AND FINANCIAL REPORTING FOR GOVERNMENTAL AND NONPROFIT ORGANIZATIONS

BASIC CONCEPTS

Robert W. Ingram
University of Alabama

Russell J. Petersen
University of Akron

Susan Work Martin
Grand Valley State University

McGraw-Hill, Inc.
New York St. Louis San Francisco Auckland Bogotá
Caracas Lisbon London Madrid Mexico City Milan
Montreal New Delhi San Juan Singapore
Sydney Tokyo Toronto

This book was set in Times Roman by the College Composition Unit
in cooperation with General Graphic Services, Inc.
The editors were Johanna Schmid and Bob Greiner;
the production supervisor was Denise L. Puryear.
The cover was designed by Carla Bauer.
R. R. Donnelley & Sons Company was printer and binder.

**ACCOUNTING AND FINANCIAL REPORTING FOR
GOVERNMENTAL AND NONPROFIT ORGANIZATIONS**
Basic Concepts

3 4 5 6 7 8 9 0 DOC DOC 9 5 4

ISBN 0-07-031714-3

Library of Congress Cataloging-in-Publication Data is available: LC Card # 90-22065.

About the Authors

ROBERT W. INGRAM is the Ernst & Young Professor of Accounting in the Culverhouse School of Accountancy at the University of Alabama. He received his Ph.D. from Texas Tech University in 1977 and is a CPA. He has contributed to numerous journal articles and to several books and monographs in the area of governmental and nonprofit accounting. He is a former Chairperson of the Governmental and Nonprofit Section of the American Accounting Association and a winner of the Section's Notable Contribution to the Literature award. He has served as a consultant with the GASB and various governmental and nonprofit organizations. He is a former editor of *Issues in Accounting Education* and is Director of Education-Elect for the American Accounting Association.

RUSSELL J. PETERSEN is Professor of Accounting and Dean of the College of Business Administration at the University of Akron. He received his Ph.D. in accounting from the University of Washington and is a CPA. He is the main author of CADRAS (Computer Assisted Data Recording and Analysis System). He has published articles and reviews in major journals dealing with topics ranging from business education to inflation accounting.

SUSAN WORK MARTIN is Associate Professor of Accounting and Taxation and the Master of Science in Taxation Program Coordinator at Grand Valley State University. She received her M.B.A. and Ph.D. in accounting from Michigan State University. She currently chairs the State of Michigan Hospital Finance Authority. She has served as the State of Michigan Commissioner of Revenue, Deputy Treasurer for Local Government Services, and as an Assistant Auditor General for a total of ten years of government experience. In recognition of her innovative tax administration, she received the 1987 Distinguished Leadership Award of the Association of Government Accountants. She is a C.P.A., C.M.A., and C.I.A. She has published articles on governmental finance topics.

Contents
in Brief

PREFACE   xiii

**Chapter 1   Introduction to Governmental and Nonprofit Accounting
              Concepts**   1

    APPENDIX 1:   GOVERNMENTAL AND NONPROFIT ACCOUNTING
                  STANDARDS   17

**Chapter 2   Understanding Governmental and Nonprofit
              Financial Reports**   27

    APPENDIX 2:   SUMMARY OF GASB FINANCIAL REPORTING
                  OBJECTIVES FOR STATE AND LOCAL
                  GOVERNMENTAL UNITS   64

Chapter 3   Using Governmental and Nonprofit Financial Reports   73

    APPENDIX 3:   AUDITING GOVERNMENTAL AND
                  NONPROFIT ORGANIZATIONS   94

Chapter 4   Understanding the Basic Accounting Cycle   102

Chapter 5   Extending the Basic Accounting Cycle   128

INDEX   165

Contents

PREFACE   xiii

**Chapter 1   Introduction to Governmental and Nonprofit Accounting
            Concepts**   1

WHAT IS A NONPROFIT ORGANIZATION?   2
HOW IS GOVERNMENTAL AND NONPROFIT ACCOUNTING AND
    REPORTING DIFFERENT?   5
THE CASE OF THE EAST RIVER HOMEOWNERS ASSOCIATION   6
GOVERNMENTAL ACCOUNTING CONCEPTS   8
    Revenues   8
    Expenditures and Expenses   9
    The Matching Concept   9
    Going Concern   10
    Assets   11
    Liabilities   12
    Accounting Entity   13
    Basis of Accounting   14
    Budgetary Control   14
ACCOUNTING PRINCIPLES FOR OTHER NONPROFIT
    ORGANIZATIONS   15
SUMMARY   16
KEY CONCEPTS AND TERMS   16
APPENDIX 1:   GOVERNMENTAL AND NONPROFIT ACCOUNTING
            STANDARDS   17
    THE ESTABLISHMENT OF GOVERNMENTAL AND NONPROFIT
        ACCOUNTING STANDARDS   17
    HISTORICAL DEVELOPMENTS IN GOVERNMENTAL
        ACCOUNTING   18
    DISCUSSION QUESTIONS   20
    EXERCISES   22
    PROBLEMS   23

Chapter 2	**Understanding Governmental and Nonprofit Financial Reports**	**27**
	FINANCIAL REPORTING OBJECTIVES AND USER INFORMATION NEEDS	27
	Accounting Controls	28
	Purposes of Financial Reporting	29
	THE STRUCTURE OF FUND ACCOUNTING	31
	Fund Accounting for State and Local Governments	31
	FUND ACCOUNTING FOR NONPROFIT ORGANIZATIONS OTHER THAN GOVERNMENTS	34
	BASIS OF ACCOUNTING FOR FUNDS	37
	Modified Accrual Accounting	37
	Flow of Financial Resources Accounting	38
	GOVERNMENT FINANCIAL REPORTING MODEL	39
	THE STATEMENT OF FINANCIAL POSITION	41
	Balance Sheets for Governmental Units	41
	Other Nonprofit Balance Sheets	45
	Summary of Balance Sheet Reporting	48
	OPERATING STATEMENTS	49
	Statements of Operating Results for Governments	49
	Operating Statements for Nonprofit Organizations Other Than Governments	54
	Summary of Reporting of Operations	57
	COMPARING BUDGETS TO ACTUAL RESULTS	58
	THE STATEMENT OF CASH FLOWS	60
	DISCLOSURES AND SCHEDULES	62
	OVERVIEW OF GOVERNMENTAL AND NONPROFIT FINANCIAL REPORTING	63
	KEY CONCEPTS AND TERMS	63
	APPENDIX 2: SUMMARY OF GASB FINANCIAL REPORTING OBJECTIVES FOR STATE AND LOCAL GOVERNMENTAL UNITS	64
	DISCUSSION QUESTIONS	65
	EXERCISES	66
	PROBLEMS	68
Chapter 3	**Using Governmental and Nonprofit Financial Reports**	**73**
	CREDITOR INFORMATION NEEDS	73
	Revenue Debt	75
	General Obligation Debt	77
	Example Financial Ratios	82
	INFORMATION FOR THIRD-PARTY DECISIONS	83
	Demonstrating Compliance	83
	Demonstrating Need and Capacity	84
	OVERSIGHT GROUP INFORMATION NEEDS	85
	INFORMATION NEEDS OF CONSTITUENTS	87

SUMMARY   90
A CASE STUDY   90
KEY CONCEPTS AND TERMS   94
APPENDIX 3:   AUDITING GOVERNMENTAL AND NONPROFIT
                     ORGANIZATIONS   94
  GOVERNMENTAL ORGANIZATIONS   94
  NONPROFIT ORGANIZATIONS   96
  DISCUSSION QUESTIONS   96
  PROBLEMS   97

Chapter 4   **Understanding the Basic Accounting Cycle**   **102**

THE BUDGETARY CYCLE   102
BUDGETARY ACCOUNTS AND ACCOUNTING PROCEDURES   103
OPERATING ACCOUNTS AND ACCOUNTING PROCEDURES   107
      Recording Taxes and Other Revenues   107
      Investment Transactions   109
      Residual Equity Transfers   109
      Interfund Loans and Transfers   110
      External and Quasi-External Transactions   112
      Intergovernmental Revenue Transactions   112
      Accounting for Expenditures and Encumbrances   113
CLOSING THE ACCOUNTS   116
ACCOUNTING FOR ACCOUNT GROUPS   117
      Acquisition and Disposal of General Fixed Assets   117
      Long-Term Debt Issuance and Payment   119
SUMMARY   122
KEY CONCEPTS AND TERMS   123
DISCUSSION QUESTIONS   123
PROBLEMS   124

Chapter 5   **Extending the Basic Accounting Cycle**   **128**

PROPERTY TAX ASSESSMENT AND COLLECTION   128
      Revenue Realization   128
      Current Classification of Receivables   131
      Liens-Subsequent Treatment of Receivables   132
CAPITAL PROJECTS   133
SPECIAL ASSESSMENTS   139
PROPRIETARY FUNDS   140
      Enterprise Funds   140
      Internal Service Funds   141
      Example Transactions   141
FIDUCIARY FUNDS   143
      Trust Funds   144
      Agency Funds   145
COMPARISON OF GOVERNMENTAL AND OTHER NONPROFIT
      ORGANIZATIONS   146

Public Schools   149
Colleges and Universities   149
Hospitals   153
Voluntary Health and Welfare Organizations   154
Other Nonprofit Organizations   156
SUMMARY   156
KEY CONCEPTS AND TERMS   157
DISCUSSION QUESTIONS   157
PROBLEMS   158

INDEX   165

Preface

The purpose of this book is to introduce students to the basic concepts of financial reporting and accounting for governmental and nonprofit organizations. It is intended to fill a gap in the current literature by providing a brief introduction to the governmental and nonprofit sector that can be integrated into existing courses. Typically, accounting courses at the principles and intermediate levels in both undergraduate and graduate programs focus almost exclusively on business organizations. This book can be used as a supplement to existing texts in order to introduce students to governmental and nonprofit accounting issues at the principles, intermediate, and advanced levels.

Students should have a grasp of the basic accounting and financial reporting concepts of business organizations before reading this book. An assumption is made in this book that students have been introduced to the basic accounting cycle and financial reports of business organizations. The concepts and principles underlying financial reporting and accounting for business organizations are compared and contrasted with those for governmental and nonprofit organizations.

The first three chapters of the book introduce the governmental and nonprofit financial reporting models. The discussion focuses on concepts rather than procedures. Chapter 1 describes differences in the political, legal, and economic environments of business and governmental and nonprofit organizations as explanations of the differences between the business and governmental and nonprofit accounting and financial reporting models. Chapter 2 explains the components of the financial reporting model giving attention to governmental and nonprofit financial statements. Chapter 3 focuses on the information needs of users of governmental and nonprofit financial reports and demonstrates how the reports can be used to meet these needs.

The last two chapters describe the accounting process underlying the financial reporting model. Chapter 4 introduces the basic accounting cycle for governmental organizations. Chapter 5 extends the discussion to include some of the more complex transactions that are typical in governmental accounting. Certain transactions of nonprofit organizations are considered as well. The discussion in these chapters is intended to be representative, not exhaustive. Students should acquire an understanding of the basics of the governmental and nonprofit financial reporting environment from this reading. A more in-depth knowledge must be acquired from further reading or course work.

The book introduces students to different types of nonprofit organizations. Reporting and accounting issues differ among these types of organizations. However, emphasis is placed on their similarities rather than on their differences. Much of the discussion focuses on governmental units because they tend to exhibit the most extreme differences from business organizations with respect to financial reporting issues.

For their helpful comments and suggestions during the preparation of this work, we wish to thank L. Charles Bokemeier, University of Kentucky; Marybeth Connolly, James Madison University; Mary Alice Seville, Oregon State University; and Mervyn W. Wingfield, James Madison University.

Robert W. Ingram
Russell J. Petersen
Susan Work Martin

ACCOUNTING AND FINANCIAL REPORTING FOR GOVERNMENTAL AND NONPROFIT ORGANIZATIONS

BASIC CONCEPTS

1

Introduction to Governmental and Nonprofit Accounting Concepts

This book deals with the financial reporting practices of state and local governments, and certain **nonprofit organizations** such as colleges and universities, hospitals, voluntary health and welfare organizations, and other entities such as religious and civic organizations. Alternatively, organizations which are primarily oriented toward providing a satisfactory rate of return to investors shall be referred to as **business organizations.** The discussion in this book assumes that the reader has an elementary understanding of the reporting practices of business organizations. Financial reporting and accounting differ in several important ways between governmental, nonprofit, and business organizations. The purpose of this book is to illustrate the important differences between these types of organizations and to describe the primary accounting concepts and practices found in governmental and nonprofit organizations.

This chapter focuses on the fundamental environmental differences between governmental, nonprofit, and business organizations. We believe that the economic, legal, and political environment of an accounting entity largely determines its accounting and reporting practices. Therefore, the goal of this chapter is to explain the environment of governmental and nonprofit organizations and to contrast it with that commonly found for business organizations. The basic accounting models of these organizations are then considered. This discussion sets the stage for examining governmental and nonprofit financial reports in Chapter 2. Chapter 3 provides a discussion of how governmental and nonprofit financial reports may be used in decision making. Finally, Chapters 4 and 5 examine accounting procedures used to collect accounting information and to prepare governmental and nonprofit financial reports. We begin this chapter by identifying the basic environmental attributes of a nonprofit organization and the major differences between the goals of nonprofit and business organizations.

WHAT IS A NONPROFIT ORGANIZATION?

Assume that as a traveler to Chicago you have flown to O'Hare International Airport, and you wish to get from the airport to downtown. You have several options, including taking a cab or taking a train. Although the two forms of transportation differ as to travel time, specific destination, and price, they both provide the same basic transportation service. However, we shall assume that one of these forms of transportation is provided by a business organization and the other is provided by a nonprofit organization.

The cab company charges individual customers a price sufficient to recover the cost of operating the cab and to pay the driver, and also to provide a satisfactory profit to the owner of the cab company. Unless the company can provide the service at a price that is acceptable to a sufficient number of customers at a profit, the cab company will not be able to operate in the long run. The competitive market in which the cab company operates provides incentives for the company to control costs and to deliver acceptable service quality. If the company is not competitive with other cab companies and with other forms of transportation, the managers will not be able to earn a sufficient return for owners on their investment in the company to make operating the cab company financially acceptable. If the stock of the cab company is traded in a public market, low rates of return will have a negative effect on the company's stock prices and likely will result in losses to investors. Such entities find reporting net income based on the concept of capital maintenance an essential feature of the accounting and reporting process in their economic environment. Capital maintenance involves identifying the return on investment earned by an organization separately from the investment.

In contrast, the train is operated as a nonprofit organization. The price of a train ticket is not necessarily set at a level that will produce a profit and recover the total costs of operating the train. Instead, the objective of the nonprofit organization may be to provide a service that is useful to a segment of the population served by the organization at a price and quality that is acceptable to the intended recipients of the service. The price and quality of service is determined primarily by a policy established by an oversight board, rather than by a competitive market.

The board could have a policy that the price of tickets should be set such that the total costs operating the train could be recovered. Such a policy would be developed to ensure that those individuals who ride the train pay for the service they receive. Alternatively, the policy could be that the price of tickets be set at a level below operating costs. Such a policy would effectively provide a subsidy from taxpayers who do not purchase tickets to those persons who do. For example, owners of businesses in downtown Chicago might be taxed to subsidize this service. Individual residential property owners also could be taxed to provide this transportation service. Both the business and residential taxpayers may benefit from the train, either as users or from increased business activity in downtown Chicago as a result of making the businesses more accessible. However, no direct relationship exists between the amount of taxes paid by a business or residential property owner and the benefits received from the train.

Unlike the cab company, the train is not owned by a specific individual or set of individuals who invest in the company. None of the service recipients or taxpayers can sell their shares in the organization. Unlike the business organization, equity interests in a nonprofit organization are obtained by voter or membership qualification and are not normally proportionate to the value of property owned or membership fees paid. Any direct benefits received by an individual taxpayer or member must come from the service provided rather than from a return on investment in the organization. Indirect benefits, such as greater access to businesses by customers, may exist, however.

The decision to form the cab company was a private decision of the owner or investors based on an expectation of earning an acceptable return by providing a service demanded by customers. The decision to provide the train service was the decision of a group of citizens that this service would benefit an important segment of the population.

Several types of benefits and goals may be realized from the existence of governmental and nonprofit organizations:

1 Governmental and nonprofit organizations may be formed so that certain services such as transportation, education, recreation, protection, or health care will be available to all residents of a community, regardless of their abilities to pay for the services.

2 Governmental and nonprofit organizations may be formed so that services that would not otherwise be available to residents, such as parks, libraries, and museums, will be available as the result of collective efforts. Frequently in this situation, these goods and services are public in nature, that is, they cannot be made available to some consumers without being made available to others. For example, a city would have difficulty in charging individual residents a price for fire or police protection. This is generally true because all residents would benefit from such services if any resident purchased them. The nonpaying residents would be **free riders** on those who did pay. This feature of a service is referred to as **separability.** Separable services can be provided to individual consumers. Unlike private goods and services, public goods and services cannot be provided to some users without, at the same time, making them available to other users.

3 Also, some governmental and nonprofit organizations exist so that certain goods and services can be made available at a lower cost than they would be if they were purchased from private businesses. This motivation has led to the formation of public utilities, transportation companies, hospitals, and similar public service organizations.

4 Nonprofit organizations may be formed because of certain common objectives that are shared by the members, as in religious or civic organizations in which the organization provides a mechanism for pooling resources for a common objective.

5 Finally, governmental organizations are formed to protect the rights and freedoms of citizens, as in the case of establishing and enforcing laws and in the case of national defense.

Thus, while both the cab company and the train provide the same basic service, the economic, legal and political environment and, therefore, the social objectives of their sponsors differ. These fundamental economic and social differences, rather than the goods or services provided, frequently distinguish a governmental or nonprofit organization from a business organization.

In summary, the following is a list of several distinguishing characteristics of a governmental or nonprofit organization:

1 It receives significant amounts of resources from providers who may not expect to receive either repayment or direct economic benefits proportionate to the resources they provide.

2 It normally has operating purposes that are other than to provide goods or services at a profit.

3 There is an absence of **defined ownership** interests that can be sold, transferred, or redeemed, or that convey entitlement to a share of a residual distribution of resources in the event of liquidation of an organization.[1]

Therefore, business organizations derive their resources from investments by owners and by sales of goods or services to customers at a price sufficient to recover operating costs and provide a return for the owners. Governmental and nonprofit organizations derive their resources from prices charged to customers, from voluntary contributions, and from involuntary contributions such as tax revenues. The various sources of revenue, together, must be sufficient to cover the cost of providing the goods or services, but an attempt ordinarily is not made to earn a profit.

We have already outlined a case which argues that many of the same goods and services can be provided by either a business or nonprofit organization. Examples include transportation, education, utilities, health care, roads, and personal protection. However, certain services are normally provided only by nonprofit organizations, particularly governments, for example, public protection and enforcement of legal rights. The primary distinguishing characteristics

---

[1]*Statement of Financial Accounting Concepts No. 4*, "Objectives of Financial Reporting by Nonbusiness Organization," Stamford, FASB, 1980, p. 3.

of a nonprofit organization are its **social purpose** and/or a lack of separability in the goods or services it provides.

HOW IS GOVERNMENTAL AND NONPROFIT ACCOUNTING AND REPORTING DIFFERENT?

Since profit-oriented businesses must operate in a market environment and report to owners who have a vested interest in earning a return on their investments, accounting reports for these organizations focus on the profitability and resources of the business entity. Whether the resources are being managed efficiently and effectively can, in part, be assessed by the owners by examining the earnings performance of the business. If the goods and services provided by the business are of the type and quality desired by customers and if the company can control the costs of providing these goods and services, the business should earn a profit such that its owners can realize a satisfactory return on their investment. If investors are not satisfied with the return that the business is providing, the business can be liquidated, or individual investors (owners) may sell their shares of the business.

In a governmental or nonprofit organization, prices of goods and services often are set by policy rather than by the forces of supply and demand. Therefore, the revenues resulting from the sale of goods and services by a governmental or nonprofit organization do not necessarily reveal the demand of users for these goods or services. In addition, costs cannot be compared to earned revenues to determine whether the operating costs of the organization are at an acceptable level. Without the mechanism of a marketplace, these organizations are at a disadvantage relative to businesses in assessing the quantity and quality of goods and services to provide. Thus, many of the unique features of governmental and nonprofit accounting and reporting result from the special needs these organizations have for controlling resources and costs and for providing accountability in the absence of market forces.

In addition to the lack of market forces, governmental organizations differ from businesses in that operating procedures and policies are heavily influenced by **legal** and **political constraints** and issues. Authority to spend may be conveyed by a legally adopted budget enacted by elected or appointed members of a governing body. Additionally, external sources of funding may come with legal constraints as to their use. Authority for action is based on laws or rules derived from a political process. Accountability is often a response to political demands rather than a response to the need for financial information that helps determine profitability. Thus, unlike business organization accounting and reporting, demonstration of compliance with laws and regulations and/ or political agendas is a major objective of governmental accounting and reporting.

Before considering governmental and nonprofit accounting concepts and practices in more detail, let's look at an example of a developing organization that will provide a basis for understanding the nature of the economic, legal, and political characteristics of a governmental or nonprofit organization.

It is important to understand that governmental and nonprofit organizations include a variety of different types of entities. Some of these entities operate similarly to business enterprises in that they sell separable goods and services to customers. Many nonprofit organizations operate auxiliary enterprises of this type. For example, college dormitories, bookstores, and cafeterias often operate as business enterprises. Local governments sometimes operate bus companies, airports, golf courses, and parking facilities as business enterprises. Many nonprofit hospitals provide the same kinds of services as hospitals that are privately owned and sell services to patients in the same manner as a profit-oriented hospital.

The discussion in this chapter focuses on comparisons and contrasts between business organizations and organizations that do not operate on a business enterprise basis. The general operations of state and local governments are examples of the nonbusiness type of organization. By focusing on examples of business organizations at one end of the spectrum and governmental, as nonbusiness, organizations at the other end of the spectrum, our discussion describes the extreme types of differences that may be observed between business and nonprofit organizations. The differences between some types of nonprofit organizations and businesses are not as extreme as those on which the discussion focuses. We will describe similarities and differences between various types of nonprofit organizations that are not as different from business enterprises as are state and local governmental units in later sections and chapters.

THE CASE OF THE EAST RIVER HOMEOWNERS ASSOCIATION

Suppose that a number of houses were built in a new residential development called East River located outside the city limits of an adjacent community. After a few years, owners of the houses formed a homeowner's association called the East River Homeowners Association (ERHA) to supervise maintenance of the area's water and sewage system and roads and to provide sanitation services. The ERHA members elected a board of directors to make necessary decisions for the membership. Over time, ERHA members began to find they needed more services than were currently provided. No fire protection was available, which made insurance rates very high. One resident had a barbecue fire go out of control, destroying part of his home before an adjacent community's fire department could respond. Traffic became a problem as many residents drove through the area at excessive speeds. Vandalism also was a nuisance. Roads needed improving to handle the increased traffic.

Many of the principal services required by ERHA, fire protection, police protection, and maintenance and improvements of roads, are jointly consumed goods which lack separability. In circumstances like these, if some of the homeowners purchase private police protection, they are providing some benefits to their neighbors as well. Police, fire, and road maintenance services are consumed jointly by all residents. It is very unlikely that many homeowners would contract individually for these services because the individual cost would be high and because the other homeowners would benefit indirectly from the services at no cost. Therefore, some type of collective political action normally is necessary to obtain these services at a reasonable cost.

The ERHA members voted to incorporate as a municipality under the name of the City of East River. Under the laws of the state and county, the new city will be entitled to assess property and sales taxes, which together with certain fees for water, will form the primary source of cash to meet service needs of residents. The city's new charter provides for a city council to be elected by the residents.

During the first year of operation, the city council hired a manager to oversee the provision of services. Employees were hired, and buildings and equipment were purchased to provide these services. Under the municipal charter, elected representatives are responsible to residents for securing sufficient resources to pay for the services. They are responsible for approving the manager's decisions to use the city's resources and for ensuring that resources are managed efficiently, effectively, and equitably. If residents are displeased with the government's performance, they can elect other representatives to the council. Legal action may be taken against council members if they are sufficiently negligent in their duties. Alternatively, residents may choose to move from the city if they believe they are being taxed unfairly or if they believe the services they are receiving are inadequate.

In summary, this example illustrates some of the primary attributes of a governmental organization such as East River:

1 The services provided are jointly consumed rather than being privately owned or they are socially desirable according to the collective wisdom of those being taxed. No particular resident has title to goods or services provided by the City and no particular resident can be excluded from receiving most of these services. A collective arrangement is required to supply services the residents desire.

2 The City is not in the "business" of selling products for a profit. Rather, the City receives resources from residents and allocates them to pay the cost of jointly consumed services. The City's objective is to allocate the scarce resources available to it to obtain the services needed by its residents at an acceptable quality and at minimum cost.

3 Individuals who reside in the City are the "owners." No purchase is made of "shares" in the City. All residents are entitled to receive services, with payments determined by property value, income, and user fees.

4 Voting rights are based on residence rather than "shares owned." All residents have one vote in the selection of management and approval of proposals, regardless of the amount of taxes and fees they pay.

The ERHA case provides a basis for examining the key concepts of nonprofit accounting, which are considered next.

GOVERNMENTAL ACCOUNTING CONCEPTS

The basic concepts of governmental accounting are examined in this section and are contrasted with profit-oriented accounting concepts. These concepts apply to those activities of governmental organizations that result in products and services that are not sold to customers as part of a business enterprise.

Revenues

In accounting for business organizations, revenues are inflows or other enhancements of assets of an entity or settlements of its liabilities from delivering or producing goods, rendering services, or other activities that constitute the entity's ongoing major or primary operations. Therefore, **business revenue** arises from the sale of products or services. The right to receive cash (accounts receivable) from sales is as legitimate a revenue as a cash receipt. On the other hand, governmental and nonprofit organization revenues arise from taxes, fees, or donations. Governmental units currently record the right to receive cash as revenue only when it is reasonably certain that the cash will be available to finance the operations of the current fiscal period.

For example, the City of East River derives revenue from property taxes assessed against residents, from sales taxes, and from certain user fees. Except for user fees, the City does not "earn" these revenues. Instead, revenues represent resources available for providing services to residents in a particular fiscal period. Thus, sales taxes often are recorded only when the cash is received by the City. Property taxes may be recorded as revenue if the payments are received during the current fiscal period or soon after the end of the period so that they are available to pay for current period services.

Business accounting does not place specific importance upon receipt of cash as a signal that revenue has occurred; it records revenue when the earnings process is essentially complete. Under generally accepted accounting principles for business organizations, revenue is recorded when it is both realizable and earned. In a practical sense this usually means that (1) no important uncertainties can exist regarding the cost to be incurred in connection with the event, and (2) cash collection of the revenue must be reasonably assured.

In contrast, most governmental revenues are not earned in the sense that they result from the direct sale of goods or services. Some taxes and fees are required of individuals without respect to usage of the services by the payor. The principal tests applied to determine whether revenue should be recorded is whether the government has a legal right to receive payment and whether the resulting financial resources will be available to finance operations of the current period. The governing board of a corporation is primarily concerned with how much revenue it has earned, whereas the governing board of a city is concerned with how much cash is available to support current services and to pay bills.

The current emphasis on availability of cash to pay current expenditures does not mean that nonprofit organizations should recognize revenues only when cash is received. Revenues should be accrued if the amount to be received can be reasonably estimated, the timing of the cash receipt is reasonably predictable, and the actions giving rise to the revenues relate to the current financial period.

Expenditures and Expenses

Expenses are outflows or other consumption of assets or incurrences of liabilities from delivering or producing goods, rendering services, or carrying out other activities that constitute the business organization's ongoing major or primary operations. The difference between revenues and expenses captures the net change in wealth that occurred from operating activities. A central notion of business accounting measurement is **capital maintenance** (distinguishing investment in a resource base from profit, return on investment in the resource base); therefore, a basic reporting requirement is to measure net income. The difference between revenues and expenses (operating income) represents the incremental change in resources that occurred from business operations after considering all expenses, including the expense resulting from the consumption of fixed assets. An objective of a business organization is to preserve the value of its resource base and to earn a profit on the use of the resource base. Expense measurement is a means of assessing decreases in the resource base that produced revenue. Only if revenues exceed expenses has capital been maintained and has profit been earned from operating activities.

Expenses often are not recorded for governmental and nonprofit organizations which are not primarily concerned with profitability and capital maintenance. Outflows of resources are called **expenditures** for these organizations and are authorized by an oversight group such as the East River City Council, based on the amount of revenues projected to be received during the fiscal period. Expenditures are recorded in the fiscal period when an obligation to be paid from currently available resources is incurred. Expenditures represent the consumption of available financial resources, not the association of expired costs with revenue. Operating, debt, and capital expenditures should be recognized when events occur that result in claims against current financial resources.

Expenditures for the City of East River are recorded when monetary resources are consumed to pay for police, fire, sanitation, road repair, and similar services. The total expenditures recorded during the fiscal year for each of these services is the total money paid out for the service plus any legal obligation incurred during the current fiscal year that will be paid from current period revenues.

The Matching Concept

A key concept in business accounting is the **matching** of revenues with associated expenses. Matching of costs and revenues refers to the simultaneous or combined recognition of revenues and expenses that result directly and jointly from the same transactions or other events. Therefore, an objective of measuring net income requires a process (1) to identify revenue and (2) to identify assets which expired in production of that revenue. This process of identifying revenue and related expired assets (expenses) utilized to produce it is called "matching."

Two broad methods are used to match revenues and expenses. First, and most desirable, is direct association of expired assets (expense) with revenue. This is often accomplished as a result of some physical event; for example, a customer taking physical possession of a product. However, many assets expire and cannot be directly associated with revenue. For example, indirect matching of the gradual expiration of long-lived assets is necessary. This indirect matching is accomplished by estimating the amount of expiration which occurred during the fiscal period. A common example of indirect matching is the depreciation of fixed assets such as buildings or machinery. This indirect matching allocates costs for the use of these resources to revenue over the course of several fiscal periods. Both methods of matching (direct and indirect) are necessary if profits are to be measured.

Matching of expenses with revenues is not a central concept or focus of accounting for many governmental and nonprofit organizations since profit measurement normally is not an objective of accounting measurement in these organizations. For governmental units, the revenues available during a fiscal period are used to pay for expenditures which are legally incurred during that period. The expenditures are not allocated against or matched with revenues. Resources which are acquired are recorded as expenditures at the point of purchase, and their costs are not allocated across fiscal periods. For example, a fire truck purchased by East River is an expenditure of the fiscal period in which it is purchased. The cost is not allocated over the useful life of the truck. Instead, the cost of the fixed asset is recorded as an expenditure when the legal obligation for payment arises.

Going Concern

The measurement of revenues and expenses to be included in the income statement of a business organization requires an assumption that the business will exist for a time period sufficient to justify the deferral process inherent in business organization accrual accounting. This assumption regarding life is usually referred to as a **going-concern** assumption and essentially means that it is expected that the business will remain in operation at least as long as the longest useful life of any of its resources or obligations. This assumption permits transactions to be recorded at values which may not represent current disposal or replacement amounts and facilitates the allocation and matching process described above. One example of the operation of the going-concern concept is the treatment of prepaid insurance as a current asset, regardless of whether or not the insurance policy has a cash redemption value. If such a policy has no value if the entity ceases operations, then it is clear that we assume that the business will be a going concern for at least as long as the period covered by the prepaid premium in order to logically justify recognition of the asset and deferral of the expense.

Alternatively, the measurement focus for recording revenues and expenditures for governmental organizations does not assume a going concern beyond the current fiscal period. The only "length of life" assumption for these organizations is that they will be able to meet payment obligations as such items become due. Again, the primary focus is on measuring revenues available to meet payment obligations of the current period and expenditures which must be paid with current period resources. In such an environment, deferrals like prepaid expenses often are not recorded. The focus is upon the immediate fiscal period. Each new year that the organization exists, it must be able to generate sufficient revenues to pay for current operating expenditures. In part, this concept is derived from a notion of equity that maintains that the recipients of services in the current period should pay for the services provided during the current period. Thus, taxpayers should not be able to tax or borrow from future generations to pay for current services. This concept is referred to as **intergenerational** or **interperiod equity.** A major exception to the application of this concept in practice is the federal government. The large deficits observed at the federal level in recent years are a violation of the intergenerational concept.

The City Council of East River is responsible for raising sufficient revenues each year to pay for the cost of services provided during the year. If sufficient revenues are not available to pay for the services desired by residents, some of the services must be eliminated or reduced. The City's ability to borrow against next year's revenues to pay for this year's services generally is constrained by law. Neither can a government raise substantially more revenues during the current year than are needed for services this period in order to pay for services in the future.

Assets

In business organization accounting, **assets** are probable future economic benefits obtained or controlled by a particular entity as a result of past transactions or events. The measurement of assets is usually determined by the unexpired cost of a resource as an estimate of its service potential. In a practical sense, an asset is usually any resource which (1) entitles the business to a legally defensible property right and (2) has service potential which extends beyond the end of the current accounting measurement period. Assets are generally measured at their historical cost (amount paid at point of purchase) less any prior fiscal period allocation of cost to revenue through the matching process. For example, a building's historical cost will appear net of depreciation expense recorded for prior fiscal periods.

Businesses segregate assets into either current (assets to be consumed in the current fiscal period) or long-term (assets which will be consumed over several fiscal periods) categories. Assets are not segregated by the source from which they were acquired. All assets are considered to be acquired to support the primary objective of generating profit.

On the other hand, governmental accounting and reporting focuses primarily on current (liquid) assets which are available to support current fiscal period services. Long-term assets may not be recorded in the operating accounts; rather, they are sometimes recorded in a separate group of accounts which serves as a "list" of what is owned, measured at original cost. The cost of such assets is not depreciated or allocated as an expense over their useful lives since the primary focus of accounting measurement in governmental organizations is the budget period, and associated issues regarding compliance with legal and political constraints within which such an organization must function. Further, since the measurement of net income, which is so central to business organization accounting, is not a goal of governmental organizations, no need exists to determine if the organization is operating in such a way as to preserve capital. Therefore, the acquisition of assets can be recorded as expenditures at the point the legal obligation for payment arises. As a separate transaction, such assets are listed in a long-term asset account group.

In summary, businesses report all assets acquired and allocate them as expenses in relationship to revenue using the matching and going-concern concepts. Governmental organizations account separately for assets available for expenditure or use in the current fiscal period from those assets which have a long-run purpose.

Liabilities

Liabilities are probable future sacrifices of economic benefits arising from present obligations of a particular entity to transfer assets or to provide services to other entities in the future as a result of past transactions or events. Also, unlike those of many nonprofit organizations, liabilities are normally viewed as obligations against the entire asset pool of a business. Assets are viewed as legally fungible, that is, one may be used in place of another; so liability obligations theoretically can be discharged through the use of any asset. Liabilities are a claim against total assets, so net worth (owner's equity) represents the net assets after subtracting liabilities.

While the concept of a liability in a governmental or nonprofit organization is quite similar to that used in business accounting, governmental accounting often focuses primarily on current assets and current liabilities; that is, assets available to support expenditures of the current period and obligations legally due for payment in the current period. Long-term obligations are to be discharged from future taxing power, grants, or donors' pledges to the entity. Only debts legally due in the current period are recorded in the operating accounts of governments. Long-term obligations are recorded in a separate group of accounts, which is a list of what is owed beyond the current period.

The account group used to maintain a record of long-term liabilities is similar in concept to the account group used to maintain a record of long-term assets which was introduced earlier.

For example, the City of East River issued long-term debt to pay for a fire truck. Since no portion of the principal or interest on the debt was paid in the current year, no obligation or expenditure associated with the debt was recorded in the operating accounts this period. An expenditure was recorded for the purchase of the truck. During the second year when interest and a portion of the principal are to be paid, a liability and expenditure for the amounts to be paid are recorded.

In summary, business liabilities represent all claims, current and long-term, against all assets. Organizations such as governments record in operating accounts only liabilities legally due in the current period to be paid from resources available within the current period.

Accounting Entity

A business financial report may include the legal entity which is formed to generate profit but also any other entities over which the primary legal entity has management control. Thus, the **accounting entity** includes all parts of the organization that are included in a common set of financial reports. For example, legally separate corporate subsidiaries whose voting stock is controlled by a parent corporation are consolidated into one financial report in business organization accounting reports. Consolidated financial reports are prepared by elimination entries to remove all duplicate items so that the resultant report is a "true" consolidated report, as if the separate entities were one. For example, intercompany loans, sales, and investments must be eliminated in preparing the consolidated report.

A financial report for state and local governments may include other entities over which the organization has significant control, in terms of management responsibility, appointment of the governing board, ability to influence operations, and accountability for fiscal matters. However, these entities are not "consolidated" into the financial report with elimination entries to remove the effect of interentity transactions. The other entities included may simply have their separate financial reports included in the organization's financial report.

For example, the financial report of the City of East River may include reports for the City School District and for a municipally owned hospital. These entities are not consolidated because different legal, political, or economic characteristics distinguish such entities from one another. These individual characteristics are important for readers of the financial report to understand.

In summary, business financial reports present all related entities as if they were one profit-generating entity. The governmental approach is to include information on entities over which the organization may have significant influence and control but not to consolidate such information.

Basis of Accounting

Businesses use the accrual basis of accounting. **Accrual** accounting attempts to recognize events as they occur and involves not only accruals but also deferrals, including allocations and amortizations. Accrual is concerned with expected future cash receipts and payments; it is the accounting process of recognizing assets and the related liabilities, revenues, expenses, gains, or losses for amounts expected to be received (or paid) in the future. The accrual basis of accounting matches expenses against revenues and allocates costs across fiscal periods through the deferral-adjustment-accrual process.

Alternatively, as discussed earlier, governmental organizations often use a hybrid form of accounting called **"modified accrual"** accounting which measures revenues when they are available to finance current expenditures. Expenditures are recognized when an obligation arises that will be paid out of current period financial resources. Rather than matching revenues earned from providing goods and services with the expired cost of providing the goods and services, governmental accounting matches financial resources available for use during a fiscal period with obligations to be paid from those resources. Accrual-deferral accounting attempts to associate revenues with the period in which they are earned and expenses with the period in which they produce revenue, while modified accrual accounting attempts to identify revenues that will be available during the current fiscal period for payment of obligations and expenditures that will be paid out of those revenues.

Budgetary Control

The degree to which budgets are utilized in businesses depends on policies established by management and the nature of the product or service being produced. Some businesses rely heavily on operating budgets for planning and control. Others do not. Factors such as complexity of the enterprise, decentralization of management decisions, size, and type of product influence budgeting. The budget is not generally a part of the financial accounting system but is instituted through a separate management control system. Budget systems are primarily influenced by management information needs rather than by the needs of investors or other external users. The degree to which a budget corresponds to actual financial results may provide information about management efficiency but has no particular legal implications. Stockholders may be disappointed if a budget projection is not met and may take action to remove management in extreme cases; however, no legal sanction is generally available for failure to meet budgetary plans.

Governmental oversight groups, such as a city council, are responsible to constituents or residents to manage the allocation of resources within legal, statutory constraints. Managers hired by oversight groups to carry out programs may be subject to personal criminal or civil action if they expend resources without budgetary authority. Accounting systems are designed to measure activities with a primary emphasis on budgetary limits. Budgetary accounts are established at the beginning of the current fiscal period and are closed at the end as a means of maintaining control over the allocation of resources.

Political constraints also influence oversight groups to use budgets to control the allocation of resources so as not to displease constituents or voters. Constituents or voters may be able to voice their opinions on the budget as a means of influencing how resources will be allocated. Budgets inform constituents about planned service activities. In addition, the budget is a benchmark against which current performance is measured. Governmental organizations normally are thought to be performing satisfactorily if they can provide an acceptable quantity and quality of services within budget limitations.

The budget is a major legal control mechanism of governmental units. In some respects, it substitutes for the market forces which determine the amount, quality, and type of goods and services produced by businesses. The budget is determined through a political process to determine the service needs of members or constituents and resources available to governmental organizations. Budgeted and actual revenues and expenditures are reported by governments in a separate financial statement.

ACCOUNTING PRINCIPLES FOR OTHER NONPROFIT ORGANIZATIONS

The discussion so far has focused on accounting principles for business organizations and, primarily, on governmental units as examples of nonprofit organizations. Accounting principles for other types of nonprofit organizations can be described in relation to businesses and governmental units and tend to fit on a continuum with businesses at one extreme and governments at the other.

For purposes of discussion, we will categorize nonprofit organizations into the following types: auxiliary enterprises, hospitals, other health and welfare organizations, colleges and universities, other nonprofit organizations, and state and local governmental units. Auxiliary enterprises are activities of governmental or nonprofit organizations (dormitories, parking facilities, cafeterias) that are operated like businesses. Accordingly, the accounting concepts for these entities are similar in most respects to those of businesses. Hospitals sell their services to patients. The services are separable; however, the patient charges may not be paid by the recipient. Third-party providers such as federal and state government agencies and insurance companies may provide much of the revenues. The price paid for the services may be set by the provider, and the services may not be provided in a competitive market. Colleges and universities charge fees to those who receive their services. However, much of the revenue comes from federal and state taxes and private donations. The services are separable but the cost of the services generally is not paid primarily by the recipient. Other nonprofit organizations include civic, social, and religious organizations. The primary source of revenues for these organizations is donations. Therefore, the revenues are not linked directly to service recipients. In many respects, these organizations are similar to governmental units except that governments have legal taxing authority.

In general, nonprofit organizations can be categorized into two groups. One group, auxiliary enterprises and hospitals, are similar to businesses with respect to many of the accounting concepts described in this chapter. They provide separable goods and services to users and receive payments based on the costs of these goods and services. The other group, public universities and health and welfare organizations, are similar to governments with respect to many of these accounting concepts. These organizations depend on taxes or contributions as major sources of funding. Accordingly, much of the cost of the services they provide is not paid by those who use the services.

SUMMARY

Businesses and many governmental and nonprofit organizations are markedly different in their fundamental economic origins, legal and political constraints, and accounting measurement concepts. Key points from this chapter include:

1 Revenues and expenses are matched in business accounting to determine net income. Monetary resource inflows and outflows are measured in governmental accounting to ensure that these resources are being used to provide for current services.

2 Legal and political considerations place greater constraints on governmental managers than on business managers, and as a result, budgetary controls are a primary focus of governmental accounting systems. Profitability is a primary control mechanism in businesses.

3 Businesses and governmental or nonprofit organizations have different economic and social objectives. Businesses attempt to earn a satisfactory return for their owners. Governmental and nonprofit organizations attempt to achieve a satisfactory quality and quantity of services with available resources.

The Appendix to this chapter examines the establishment of financial accounting standards for governmental and nonprofit organizations. The next chapter examines the financial reports of these organizations.

KEY CONCEPTS AND TERMS

Governmental organization
Nonprofit organization
Business organization
Separability
Market
Defined ownership
Social purpose

Investment
Rate of return
Political constraints
Legal constrains
Business voting rights
Nonprofit organization voting rights
Business revenue

Nonprofit revenue
Expenditure
Expense
Capital maintenance
Matching
Going concern
Intergenerational equity
Interperiod equity
Asset

Liability
Accounting entity
Accrual
Modified accrual
Budgetary control—nonprofit organization
Budgetary control—business organization

APPENDIX 1: Governmental and Nonprofit Accounting Standards

THE ESTABLISHMENT OF GOVERNMENTAL AND NONPROFIT ACCOUNTING STANDARDS

A major factor influencing governmental and nonprofit accounting practices centers on the way in which accounting standards are established and on the groups that have responsibility for setting the standards. The Financial Accounting Standards Board (FASB) is charged with the establishment of standards of reporting for businesses and for certain nonprofit organizations. The Securities and Exchange Commission (SEC) is the body which has legal authority to promulgate and impose standards on private enterprises which issue publicly traded securities. The SEC has allowed the private sector, through the FASB, to set accounting and financial reporting standards for private sector enterprises. Thus, standards exist which apply uniformly to all publicly traded corporations operating in the U.S. economy. SEC authority does not extend to governmental and nonprofit organizations.

Governmental and nonprofit organizations exist in a variety of political and legal settings. For example, local governments are governed by the laws of the state in which they exist, which vary substantially among states. The purposes for which governmental and nonprofit organizations exist vary substantially as well. These include such widely diverse activities as health care and college education.

Some unifying themes exist in governmental and nonprofit financial reporting. The American Institute of Certified Public Accountants (AICPA) has prepared a series of Audit Guides as aids to financial reporting and auditing, which have established, to some degree, uniformity in accounting practice in certain limited areas. Prior to 1985, the National Council on Governmental Accounting (NCGA) published a series of Statements providing guidance for financial reporting by state and local governments. The Governmental Accounting Standards Board (GASB) was established in 1984 as a further effort to bring uniformity to governmental financial reporting.

The GASB functions in a manner similar to the FASB. Both Boards report to the Financial Accounting Foundation which is responsible for selecting Board members and for raising funds to support the Boards. The GASB has five members: a full-time chairman, a full-time member/research director, and three part-time members. The GASB has responsibility for governmental accounting standards at the state and local level (the federal government sets its own standards), while the FASB is responsible for nonprofit organizations that are not controlled by a governmental unit.

Other organizations such as the Health Care Financial Management Association, the American Hospital Association, and the National Association of College and University Business Officers have played a role in the determination of accounting practices for their respective nonprofit organizations. This diverse organizational environment explains some of the diversity in governmental and nonprofit accounting standards.

HISTORICAL DEVELOPMENTS IN GOVERNMENTAL ACCOUNTING

In 1934 the Municipal Finance Officers Association (MFOA) moved into the forefront in the accounting standard setting process for local governments by creating the National Committee on Municipal Accounting. The committee was renamed the National Committee on Governmental Accounting in 1949. In 1974 it was again renamed the National Council on Governmental Accounting (NCGA) and issued Statements and Technical Interpretations until June 1984, when the GASB commenced operations in Stamford, Connecticut. The GASB was formed after two years of hearings, negotiations, and compromise between various public interest groups. The GASB is now the official issuer of GAAP (generally accepted accounting principles) for state and local governmental entities. The GASB, along with the FASB, moved to Norwalk, Connecticut, in 1989.

The existence of the GASB depends on the support of the numerous public sector organizations that support it and agree voluntarily to adopt its standards. Jurisdictional issues have continued to arise between the FASB and the GASB. These issues pertain primarily to types of organizations which may operate in either public or private sectors such as hospitals and universities. The major problem to be resolved is whether accounting standards should be uniform across all organizations controlled by governmental units, including public hospitals and universities, or whether accounting standards should be uniform across all entities of a similar purpose, that is, all hospitals should follow the same standards. In 1989, the jurisdictional issue was resolved (at least temporarily) in favor of the GASB being the appropriate standard-setting body for all organizations controlled by governmental units, including government-operated hospitals and universities.

In 1968, the NCGA issued an authoritative publication, *Governmental Accounting, Auditing and Financial Reporting,* commonly referred to as GAAFR or the "blue book." It was basically a "how-to-record" manual; that is, how to record property taxes, how to record receipts from collections, appropriations, etc. The 1968 GAAFR was a fundamental accounting manual for the local government finance officer and served as an instructional manual for preparing accounting records. The 1968 GAAFR assumed a prominent role in establishing accounting guidance for governmental units. The GAAFR was revised in 1980 to incorporate NCGA Statements 1 and 2 and was revised again in 1988.

In 1974, the AICPA issued an audit guide, *Audits of State and Local Governmental Units* (ASLGU). The audit guide affirmed the 1968 GAAFR as constituting generally accepted accounting principles for state and local governments, except as otherwise modified in the guide. The guide provided explanation, interpretation, and application of certain principles which went beyond GAAFR.

The AICPA issued two *Statements of Position* which further modified GAAP for governments in 1975 and 1977: *Statement of Position No. 75-3*, "Accrual of Revenues and Expenditures by State and Local Governmental Units," and *Statement of Position No. 77-2*, "Accounting for Interfund Transfers of State and Local Governmental Units." In 1978 the AICPA issued the second edition of the industry audit guide which included *Statement of Position No. 75-3* and *No. 77-2*. A revised edition was issued in 1986.

In 1975, the Office of Revenue Sharing was established by the federal government to administer federal revenue sharing to state and local governments. The enabling legislation contained a requirement that audits be performed no less than every three years. For the first time, all state and local governments receiving more than $25,000 in federal revenue sharing funds were required to have an audit in conformance with generally accepting auditing standards. Since the audit is GAAP based, incentives are provided by this requirement for governmental units to adopt GAAP for financial reporting purposes. The revenue sharing act was recently amended to provide that all recipients of $100,000 or more must have an annual audit. "The Single Audit Act of 1984," signed into law October 19, 1984, required each unit of government receiving more than $100,000 in federal aid to obtain an annual or biennial independent audit of operations. Under this Act, a single audit is sufficient for all federal aid programs if the audit meets federal guidelines.

In 1979, the NCGA made a significant change in the financial reporting model by issuing *Statement No. 1*, "Governmental Accounting and Financial Reporting Principles," and *Statement No. 2*, "Grant, Entitlement and Shared Revenue Reporting by State and Local Governments." These statements increased the extent to which financial statements of funds were combined in financial statement presentations. These statements were effective for fiscal years ending on or after June 30, 1980.

In 1980, Standard & Poors, a bond rating agency, issued a *Policy Statement on Municipal Accounting and Financial Reporting* which required accounting and reporting in accordance with GAAP. It also required that financial statements be issued no later than six months after fiscal year-end. Noncompliance with this policy statement could result in a negative effect on the governmental unit's bond rating or a decision not to rate the unit's bonds. The rating agency policy provided an incentive for governments to issue audited statements in compliance with GAAP.

In 1980, the MFOA, which later became the Government Finance Officers Association (GFOA), issued a revised edition of the GAAFR. It was not intended as an authoritative pronouncement of GAAP; however, it was intended to provide guidance to effectively apply NCGA *Statement No. 1* principles. The 1980 GAAFR addressed areas which were not discussed in *Statement No. 1* or *No. 2*, so by default assumed some authoritativeness on those issues. The NCGA continued to issue specific interpretations and Statements on issues, such as the timing of recognition of property taxes and definition of the reporting entity, before terminating in June 1984.

In 1980, the FASB issued *Statement of Financial Accounting Concepts No. 4*, "Objectives of Financial Reporting by Nonbusiness Organizations." In 1981, the NCGA issued *Statement of Accounting and Financial Reporting Objectives of Governmental Units*. Both documents attempted to establish a conceptual basis for the development of accounting standards.

In 1981, an ad hoc committee issued a *Report of the Governmental Accounting Standards Board Organization Committee* (GASBOC) which proposed an independent standards board for governmental GAAP. The final report was issued on October 13, 1981, and the GASB commenced operation in June 1984, taking over from the NCGA.

In 1986, the AICPA issued a revised Audit Guide for state and local governmental units (ASLGU). It reflected reporting formats in conformance with NCGA *Statement No. 1* and updated the entire 1978 ASLGU. Also, the AICPA adopted a policy that made GASB standards authoritative under Rule 203 of its code of ethics. Independent CPAs are required to examine financial reports for compliance with GASB pronouncements when issuing an audit opinion.

The GASB issued *Statement No. 1* in 1986 which affirmed existing NCGA and AICPA standards as constituting GAAP for governments until subsequently modified by GASB Statements. Current GAAP for governmental entities consists of GASB Statements as well as AICPA *Statements of Position Nos. 75-3, 77-2, 80-2* and the AICPA accounting and auditing guides:

Audits of Certain Nonprofit Organizations, 2d ed., 1987.
Audits of Colleges and Universities, 2d ed., 1975.
Audits of State and Local Governmental Units, rev. ed., 1986.
Audits of Voluntary Health and Welfare Organizations, 2d ed., 1988.
Hospital Audit Guide, 6th ed., 1985.

One of the accomplishments of the GASB has been to issue the *Codification of Governmental Accounting and Financial Reporting Standards* that provides a comprehensive source of GAAP for state and local governments. The *Codification* is updated periodically for new pronouncements.

DISCUSSION QUESTIONS

1 List three organizations that operate as governmental or nonprofit entities and describe their principal objectives and economic, legal, and political environments.
2 List three organizations that operate as business entities, and describe their principal objectives and economic, legal, and political environments.

3 Identify one public service provided by a governmental or nonprofit organization in which lack of separability is the principal justification for not providing the service through a business organization.

4 Identify one public service provided by a governmental or nonprofit organization in which a socially desirable service is the principal justification for not providing the service through a business organization.

5 What is the principal focus of accounting reports developed to describe a business organization? Why is this focus useful and accepted in society?

6 What is the principal focus of accounting reports developed to describe a governmental or nonprofit organization? Why is this focus useful and accepted in society?

7 How is the price for a product or service determined in markets served by a business organization?

8 How are revenues determined in a governmental or nonprofit organization?

9 Contrast the meaning of the term "efficiency" as it applies to nonprofit and business organizations.

10 "Profit maximization" and "constrained cost minimization" are each terms which are sometimes used to describe objectives of either a business or a nonprofit organization. Define each and discuss why these objectives are frequently driven by political, legal, and economic considerations.

11 Define "ownership" in a business organization and contrast the concept with "ownership" in a governmental or nonprofit organization.

12 To whom is the manager in a business organization primarily accountable?

13 To whom is the manager in a nonprofit organization primarily accountable?

14 What sanctions does society impose on inefficient management performance in a business organization?

15 What sanctions does society impose on inefficient management performance in a governmental or nonprofit organization?

16 Discuss and contrast the accounting concept of revenue as it is used in business and governmental organizations.

17 How does the concept of an expense in a business organization differ from the accounting concept of an expenditure in a governmental organization?

18 Capital maintenance is a central theme in business accounting concepts. Does it apply in nonprofit accounting? Why or why not?

19 Matching is an accounting concept fundamental to business entity income measurement. How does the concept apply to a governmental or nonprofit accounting system?

20 A pervasive underlying concept in business accounting measurement is the going concern. Describe going concern as it applies to business accounting, and discuss the application of the same idea in governmental accounting.

21 The deferral-adjustment-accrual process is basic to the realignment of cash flows in business accounting for the purpose of calculating net income. How do these notions apply in governmental and nonprofit accounting conventions and practices?

22 Contrast the meaning of the term "asset" in business and in governmental accounting reports.

23 Liabilities are thought to be claims against total assets in business accounting. In governmental accounting a different concept of liabilities sometimes exists. Describe this concept.

24 Contrast accrual and modified accrual accounting concepts as they apply to the identification of revenues.

25 Budgets are an important device in financial accounting for some governmental and nonprofit entities. Why is this the case?

26 How does a business entity utilize a budget? Why is a budget in a business entity not reported as part of its external financial statements?

EXERCISES

1 White Company is a publisher of periodicals. In 19X1 White took subscriptions for $150,000 to be delivered in equal amounts during 19X2 and 19X3. What amount of revenue would White properly recognize during 19X2 and 19X3 from subscriptions? Why?

2 Stone City is a small municipality. Stone's primary source of revenues is from a sales tax levied on retail sales within the city limits. During 19X1 Stone's accountant estimates that $150,000 in taxes will be levied and that 70 percent will be received from merchants in 19X1 and 30 percent in 19X2 based on retail sales in the City during 19X1. What amount of tax revenue should be reported to the City Council for 19X1? Why? What factors affect this decision?

3 Brown Company is a small logging company. In early 19X1, Brown purchases 10 new logging trucks for a total expenditure of $750,000. Brown gives a 10 percent cash down payment and signs a simple interest, 10 percent five-year note payable for the balance. The trucks have a five-year useful life and are expected to have no salvage value at the end of their life. How should Brown account for the trucks and the loan during 19X1? Why?

4 Moss City provides a refuse pickup service for its residents. The City Council authorizes the purchase of 10 new refuse trucks at a total purchase price of $750,000 near the end of 19X1 from 19X1 revenues. The trucks are delivered in early 19X2. How would these transactions be treated by Moss City in 19X1 and 19X2? Why?

5 Green Manufacturing Company realizes $450,000 in revenue during 19X1 from the sale of 150,000 computer disks. The company began the year with 10,000 disks on hand at a unit cost of $2.10 and purchased 145,000 disks during the year for $2.10 per disk. What should Green report as gross profit for 19X1 on these transactions? How does the matching concept operate in this situation as an aid to determining gross profit?

6 Cotton City is a large municipality. During 19X1, Cotton has budgeted and expended $435,000 for the purchase of 145,000 computer disks for use in its administrative activities. Cotton began 19X1 with 10,000 disks on hand which cost the City $3.00 each. During the year, 150,000 disks were used by city employees. How should Cotton City account for these costs? Why?

7 During 19X1, Gold Manufacturing Company budgeted for $1,300,000 of expenses. Actual expenses amounted to $1,375,000. The company produced and sold the amount of product it originally budgeted. How does the difference between actual and budgeted expense affect the decisions made by Gold's managers?

8 Wheat City has a planned total expenditure of $1,192,500 for 19X1. Actual expenditures for 19X1 turned out to be $1,290,000. How is this budget variance important for city officials? How does it affect the decisions they must make?

9 Blue's Company is a manufacturer of computer components. At the end of 19X1 Blue's purchasing manager places an order for $250,000 to acquire 125,000 electronic components. The components are delivered in early 19X2 at an actual cost of

$260,000. When should the Company record the acquisition of the electronic components in its inventory and record the liability for their purchase? When should the components be treated as an expense to be associated with revenue through the matching process?

10 Timber County places an order for a planned expenditure of $250,000 at the end of 19X1 to be paid out of 19X1 revenues. The items ordered are delivered in 19X2. In which year would the use of financial resources and liability associated with the purchase be reported? Why?

PROBLEMS

1 Suppose that some of the residents of the City of East River are concerned about providing transportation for residents to and from a nearby larger community, Valley City. Since East River does not have any shopping facilities or schools, frequent trips are required between East River and Valley City. Some of the residents feel that it would be possible to form a bus company to provide this service, and also to provide an opportunity for a profitable investment for potential stockholders. Accordingly, the group seeks legal and accounting advice which leads to the establishment of a corporate business organization called North St. Bus Company in late November 19X1. Common stock is made available to residents of East River at $10 per share. While not all residents elect to participate in this investment, $50,000 in cash is received in issuance of common stock by the end of December 19X1. The company also is able to borrow $100,000 on a five-year, 12 percent note from Valley City State Bank. The principal of the note is payable in five equal installments together with interest on December 31, of each year. With these resources available, the company acquires two 20-passenger buses for $20,000 each in early January 19X2. The City rents a small building in which to house the buses and perform maintenance. Employees are hired to drive the buses, provide maintenance and administrative services, and North begins offering passenger services during January 19X2. The following data summarize transactions of the North St. Bus Company for 19X2:

Fare revenue	$325,000
Rent expense	12,000
Payment of principal	20,000
Interest expense	12,000
Salaries expense	150,000
Fuel expense	152,000
Maintenance expense	7,000
Insurance expense	4,000
Supplies expense	2,500

Other items relevant to this year's operations include:

- The Company agreed to provide services on a monthly ticket basis. Included in Fare Revenue above is $10,000 for monthly ticket fees received in 19X2 for services to be provided in January 19X3.
- Salaries unpaid and unrecorded at the end of 19X2 for services rendered in December were $750.
- Unpaid fuel bills on December 31 were $12,000.

- The insurance policies purchased were two-year policies expiring December 31, 19X3.
- Supplies on hand at the end of 19X2 cost $900.
- The life of the buses is estimated to be five years with $5000 salvage value.

Required

a Prepare summary journal entries to record the transactions listed above through December 31, 19X2. Prepare an income statement and a statement of retained earnings for 19X2 and a balance sheet as of December 31, 19X2, for North St. Bus Company.

b What is North St. Bus Company's principal purpose? Have the principal purposes of the investors in this company been met as a result of their investment?

2 Refer to Problem 1 above. Assume that when the stock issue was offered to the residents of the City, very few residents were interested in the investment. Most felt that others would commit to support the bus company, and that they would therefore benefit in increased convenience and enhanced property values as a result of the establishment of the bus line without the commitment of an initial investment. After some frustration, the persons organizing the bus line prepared a proposal for a city-owned bus line, including a budget and submitted it to the City Council of East River.

The budget submitted for the first year's operations reflected the following information:

Planned cash receipts:	
Special tax levy	$ 50,000
Issue note	100,000
Fare revenue	100,000
General tax revenues	230,000
Planned cash disbursements:	
Purchase buses	40,000
Rent	12,000
Payment of principal	20,000
Payment of interest	12,000
Salaries	148,000
Fuel	150,000
Maintenance	8,000
Insurance	4,500
Supplies	2,000

Those proposing the establishment of the bus service as a municipal project made their case to the City Council on the following major arguments:

- That there would be a general enhancement of property values, of benefit to all residents in East River, as a result of the establishment of bus service to Valley City.
- That many of the residents of East River were elderly and only marginally able to transport themselves to Valley City for shopping and medical care. The es-

tablishment of the bus service would be of great benefit to these members of the East River community.
• That many of the children living in East River attended school in Valley City. The establishment of a bus line would provide an enhanced device for these children to travel to and from school. Also, many of these children were active in school and Valley City community programs at other than school hours. The bus system would also contribute to solving this transportation problem.

The proposal called for a special-purpose tax levy on residents which would raise $50,000 during late December 19X1. The organizers assured the Council that with this level of commitment, the Valley City State Bank would loan an additional $100,000 to get the project under way. The group argued that due to the general beneficial nature of the bus system, the transportation should be offered at less than direct cost. This proposal would require that the residents of East River subsidize the bus line with a general tax to be levied each year on property for all residents. After some deliberation, the Council decided to go forward with the project and levied the tax in late 19X1. Tax collections in the amount of $50,000 were received by the end of December. Actual cash receipts and disbursements for 19X2 were as follows:

Receipts:	
Issue note	$100,000
Fare revenue	98,000
Property tax revenues	227,000
Disbursements:	
Purchase buses	40,000
Rent	12,000
Payment of principal	20,000
Payment of interest	12,000
Salaries	148,000
Fuel	155,000
Maintenance	7,400
Insurance	4,500
Supplies	2,200

Required

a What are the principal economic, political, and social circumstances of the East River Bus Line? How do these differ from those of the North St. Bus Company described in Problem 1?

b Make a list of accounting practices that will differ between East River Bus Line and North St. Bus Company. Make a list of accounting practices that will be similar.

c What is East River Bus Line's principal purpose? Have the objectives of the residents of East River been met as a result of the establishment of this service?

d Develop an accounting system to account for the transactions of East River Bus Line. Prepare a statement that compares revenues and expenditures for the bus line using your best judgment as to how this information should be prepared.

3 Suppose that Druid Cooperative began operations in late 19X1 with the issuance of no-par common stock in exchange for $500,000. The Coop is a farming supply organization and follows the usual business accounting practice of realizing revenue when the products that it sells to customers are delivered. It is quite common for farming supply companies to agree to payment deferral until the crops that are harvested by its customers are brought to market. Under this arrangement, Druid sold $150,000 in seeds for cotton to its customers in late 19X1 which were purchased earlier in 19X1 by Druid with a single cash payment of $75,000. The actual receipt of cash for this sale was received in October 19X2. The only other expenses that Druid incurred in 19X1 were depreciation on a storage building purchased in 19X1 for $200,000 which has a life of 20 years and no salvage value (assume straight line depreciation), annual salaries of $50,000, and utilities of $25,000. All salaries and utilities were paid in cash by the end of the year. Purchase orders for supplies not yet received in the amount of $10,000 were outstanding at the end of 19X1.

Required

a Prepare an income statement for Druid Cooperative for the year ended December 31, 19X1, and a balance sheet as of December 31, 19X1.

b Under the assumption that Druid is not a business organization but that it is a governmental organization which has been established to support farming operations in Druid County, answer each of the following questions:

(1) If the $500,000 had been received as a result of a special tax levy, how might the receipt of the cash have been reported in 19X1 and 19X2?

(2) If the $150,000 in receipts was generated as a tax based on a millage rate applied to the tons of cotton harvested, how might the distribution of seeds and the receipt of cash in 19X1 and 19X2 have been treated from an accounting and reporting perspective?

(3) If the Druid County Commission requires the company to record budgets, how might this requirement impact on the accounting records? Contrast this practice with that usually followed by business organizations.

(4) How would Druid County report the other costs listed above for salaries and utilities in 19X1 and 19X2?

(5) How would the outstanding purchase order for supplies affect Druid County's financial condition for 19X1 and 19X2? What concerns should the County Commission have about this item?

2

Understanding Governmental and Nonprofit Financial Reports

Chapter 1 reviewed accounting concepts that are common to both business and governmental/nonprofit organizations. The chapter also summarized some of the primary differences in accounting concepts between the two types of organizations. It is important to keep these concepts and differences in mind as we examine governmental and nonprofit financial reports. While the reports are similar in many respects to those of business enterprises, a number of differences exist. These differences arise because the economic, legal, and political environments in which different types of organizations exist lead to different user information needs.

The purpose of this chapter is to illustrate the primary financial reports issued by governmental and nonprofit organizations. This chapter describes the format and content of the reports and discusses how the reports relate to the concepts examined in Chapter 1.

The next section of this chapter provides an overview of governmental and nonprofit financial reporting objectives and user information needs. The remainder of the chapter examines financial statements and disclosures. Emphasis is placed on the differences between governmental financial reports and those of business enterprises.

FINANCIAL REPORTING OBJECTIVES AND USER INFORMATION NEEDS

Recall from Chapter 1 that business and governmental/nonprofit organizations differ in several key ways. Businesses operate in market environments and provide goods and services demanded by consumers in an attempt to earn a return (profit) for investors. Governmental and nonprofit organizations frequently provide goods and services outside of a competitive market environment and normally do not seek to earn a return for investors. The financial objective of these organizations is usually to provide the goods and services desired by their constituents at a satisfactory level of quality and at a reasonable cost.

Accounting Controls

While a primary objective of financial reporting for business enterprises is to inform investors about the risk and potential return they can expect from their investments, governmental reports emphasize the allocation of resources to provide services within legal and political constraints. Since competitive market forces frequently are not present for governmental and nonprofit organizations to the extent they are for businesses, other (nonmarket) control mechanisms often are implemented to encourage efficient and effective resource management and to assure compliance with legal requirements. The accounting system in governmental and nonprofit accounting often provides the means by which many of these controls are implemented.

For example, several controls may be observed in governmental and nonprofit financial statements. The following are particularly important and will be emphasized in the description of financial statements in the later sections of this chapter.

Funds Control   Unlike business organizations which operate as a single accounting entity, governmental and some nonprofit organizations separate resources into multiple accounting entities, called "funds," to reduce the opportunity for managers to use resources designated for one purpose for some other purpose. Funds also provide a convenient means of describing for readers the resources that are available for specific purposes and how the resources have been used.

Expenditure Control   Governmental and many nonprofit organizations do not "earn" a major portion of their revenues in a business sense. Instead revenues are obtained by requiring constituents to pay taxes or from receiving donations to cover current operating requirements. Accordingly, financial statements focus on expendable resources that have been obtained during the current fiscal year. These expendable resources are compared with the uses of these resources to ensure that managers are not overspending or building unnecessary surpluses. Also, financial statements segregate currently expendable resources from other sources. Obligations that are to be paid or that have been paid from currently expendable resources are also segregated from other obligations.

Budgetary Control Management discretion over the use of resources may be limited by legally adopted budgets that specify how resources are to be obtained and used. Comparisons of budgeted and actual revenues and expenditures are made for some entities, primarily governments, to ensure that this legal requirement is being met.

Other control mechanisms exist within the accounting system that relate to the way data are collected and summarized. These mechanisms are described in later chapters.

Purposes of Financial Reporting

The primary purpose of financial reports is to provide information useful to those interested in an organization's financial performance. Management control is only one dimension of information useful to governmental and nonprofit organizations and their constituents. Other purposes similar to those for businesses include:

1 Reporting the *stock of resources* available to an organization and claims to those resources

2 Reporting the *flow of resources* through an organization, where the resources were obtained, and how they were used

3 Disclosing *sufficient information about the financial activities* of an organization to reliably gauge resources, obligations, and resource flows

Formal statements of the objectives of financial reporting by governmental and nonprofit organizations have been issued by accounting standard setting organizations. These objectives are summarized in the Appendix to this chapter. The objectives of financial reports indicate the needs of various users of the reports.

Similarities and differences exist in the objectives of governmental or nonprofit and business reports because similarities and differences exist in the needs of users of these reports and in the economic, political, and legal circumstances of these two forms of organization. For example, we have stated that equity investors do not exist for governmental or nonprofit organizations in the usual financial sense. "Investors" in the context of a governmental or nonprofit organization are the electorate or membership group for whom the organization exists. While such a group does not "invest" in the organization directly, it does hold a legally enforceable interest in the affairs of the organization. Also, creditors do exist and the needs of these users are similar to creditors of business organizations. Creditors are primarily concerned with whether an organization will be able to meet debt service (payment of principal and interest) requirements on a timely basis. Various funds, accounts, and disclosures of governmental and nonprofit organizations are designed for the needs of creditors and are illustrated later in the chapter.

Like boards of directors of business organizations, governmental and nonprofit organizations have boards or councils who are elected by the organizations' supporters or constituents to supervise management's financial decisions. These oversight groups for governmental and nonprofit organizations may take a more direct role in financial management than do their corporate counterparts because of the political circumstances of a governmental or nonprofit organization. For example, city councils approve budgets and pass ordinances that may have a direct impact on a city's finances. Members of governmental and nonprofit organization boards and councils sometimes have little experience or training in financial management and frequently are very sensitive to the political implications of their decisions.

Resources for governmental and nonprofit organizations are often provided by grants from other organizations. These granting organizations may evaluate the financial needs of a recipient and the efficiency and effectiveness of its management when deciding whether grants should be made or renewed. In addition, many granting organizations wish to be sure that grants are used by a recipient in compliance with the grant requirements. Financial reports frequently serve this reporting and accountability need.

Numerous other users may exist for governmental and nonprofit financial reports. Taxpayers, employees, donors, service recipients, and suppliers are a few examples. However, the information needs of these groups are less specifically linked to the financial operations of an organization than are those of the other users mentioned. Accordingly, the format and content of governmental and nonprofit financial reports currently are structured primarily to serve the needs of creditors, oversight groups, and granting organizations.

Less uniformity and agreement about the format and content of financial reports for different governmental and nonprofit organizations exists than for business financial reports. This lack of uniformity results, historically, from the lack of a single professional accounting standard setting body like the FASB which establishes reporting standards for business organizations. Indeed, the existence of several professional organizations which have influenced the format of the statements and the large variety of purposes for which the statements may be used are major contributory factors to the diversity in nonprofit financial reporting. The description in this chapter reflects a composite of the recommendations of various organizations that have provided guidelines for nonprofit financial reporting. These guidelines are not always observed in every practice situation. The description in this chapter is a general illustration of what one might observe in actual financial reports.

Governmental organizations may publish more than one type of annual financial report. A **comprehensive annual financial report** (CAFR) is required by the GASB to be in conformance with generally accepted accounting principles. This report contains a complete set of financial statements and disclosures including a set of **general-purpose financial statements** (GPFS). The GPFS contain less detail and may be published for general public use apart from a CAFR. Differences in the content of these two report forms will be described later. First, the next section examines the structure of accounting funds.

THE STRUCTURE OF FUND ACCOUNTING

A **fund** is an accounting and fiscal (controls money) entity with its own set of accounts segregated for the purpose of carrying on a specific activity, usually within legal limitations. Why do we have funds in governmental and nonprofit accounting? Fund accounting attempts to control the use of resources by placing them in separate accounting entities (funds) according to the purpose for which they are to be used. For example, the executive branch of a government is charged with carrying out activities as directed by the legislative branch. The legislative branch appropriates (that is, authorizes spending) money to be used by the executive branch to carry out the directed activities. To ensure accountability and that no one overspends beyond the amount appropriated, separate funds are established for major types of activities and to separate resources which may be used for current general operations from those that are restricted for specific purposes. Each fund is a separate accounting entity, with its own set of accounts, which exists to control and report a subset of the activities of an organization. A fund segregation of resources does not, by itself, establish an infallible system of internal control. Nevertheless, along with other controls, fund accounting prevails as part of the basic control framework of governmental and nonprofit accounting.

Fund Accounting for State and Local Governments

The discussion in this section focuses first on fund accounting for state and local governments. Fund accounting for other nonprofit organizations is similar in many respects to that of governments and will be discussed later in this chapter. Some governments have used hundreds of funds in their accounting systems. The GASB strongly recommends that governments minimize the number of funds utilized and identifies seven fund types divided into three categories: (1) governmental, (2) proprietary, and (3) fiduciary.[1] Each of these fund types is discussed below.

Governmental Funds   Governmental Funds account for activities supported by general government revenues such as taxes and include the General, Special Revenue, Capital Projects, and Debt Service Funds.

The General Fund   The General Fund accounts for the operations of the government that are paid for out of general revenues. **General revenues** are those sources of income which can be used for the current general operations of the government. Therefore, these revenues are not restricted for a special purpose. General public services can be supported with these revenues. The General Fund is normally used to account for all activities not accounted for in

---

[1]GASB *Codification of Governmental Accounting and Financial Reporting Standards,* Section 1100.103.

other funds. Major services such as police, fire, and sanitation generally are paid for from the General Fund. The General Fund may also be the source of financial resources for activities accounted for in other funds. For example, the General Fund may provide the resources for construction of a new city hall, but a Capital Projects Fund (described below) will account for the construction activity itself to provide more detailed accountability and control.

Special Revenue Funds Special Revenue Funds account for activities in which revenue is legally designated for a specific purpose. For example, gasoline taxes may be legally designated to support only road maintenance and no other governmental activity. In such a situation, a Special Revenue Fund would be established to receive and disburse these resources.

Capital Projects Funds Capital Projects Funds account for construction or acquisition of major capital facilities financed by general government revenues. The balance of the Capital Projects Fund generally reverts to the General Fund or Debt Service Fund upon completion of the project, and then the fund is closed.

Debt Service Funds Debt Service Funds account for payment of principal and interest on general long-term debt, debt to be repaid from general revenues. Debt service activities also may be accounted for in the fund financing the payments, usually the General Fund. A separate Debt Service Fund is often legally required when obligations are issued, to assure the bondholder that money for repayment will be segregated and safeguarded.

Proprietary Funds Proprietary Funds are used to account for goods and services that are sold to consumers of the goods and services and include Enterprise and Internal Service Funds.

Enterprise Funds Enterprise Funds account for the activities of a business-type entity that is operated by a government. A common example of an Enterprise Fund would be a government-owned utility which might exist to provide water or some other service or product. The product of the utility can be sold to individual consumers since the amount of the product used by each consumer can be measured. Thus, these goods are separable among individual consumers. A capital maintenance focus is possible for this type of fund since the product can be sold at a price that will permit the enterprise to continue as a going concern. The expenses associated with operating the enterprise can be compared with the revenues generated by selling the product. Enterprise Funds are created to account for service activities which are sold primarily to users outside the governmental entity. Since enterprise services are sold to customers, and the goal of such organizations is usually to recover cost, or possibly even to earn a profit, accounting for these activities is similar to accounting for business enterprises.

Internal Service Funds Internal Service Funds account for the activities of a division within the governmental unit that sells goods and services to other divisions. A common example of an Internal Service Fund is a motor pool.

Other examples would be a central stores and supplies division, a data processing service, and an employee cafeteria. Internal Service Funds are accounted for based on concepts typically used to account for a business enterprise, but the objective is normally to recover cost (to break even) rather than to earn a profit. In situations like these, the cost of producing the service should approximately equal user charges.

Fiduciary Funds Fiduciary Funds account for resources that are restricted in use by someone external to the government. The government does not have primary control over the use of the resources but is responsible for them. Fiduciary funds include Trust and Agency Funds.

Trust and Agency Funds Trust and Agency Funds account for assets held by the government for another entity either as a trustee or agent. A trustee manages resources that belong to or are maintained for someone else, for example, resources for employee retirement. An agent takes the place of someone else for a specific purpose, for example, collection of taxes. Four types of Trust and Agency Funds are as follows:

1 Expendable Trust Funds may expend both principal (resources held in trust) and interest accumulated from investing the principal for their designated objectives. They commonly expend resources transferred to them from nonexpendable trust funds. For example, a donation to purchase books for a library may be placed in a Trust Fund. The donation is invested until it is needed to purchase books.

2 Nonexpendable Trust Funds may not expend trust principal. Investment earnings may be transferred to an expendable trust fund for expenditure according to the specified purpose of the trust. For example, a donation to endow a scholarship at a university would be placed in a Trust Fund. The earnings from investment of the endowment would be used to provide scholarships, but the endowment itself would not be spent.

3 Pension Trust Funds account for public employee retirement system activities. The employer retains and invests employee and employer contributions according to specified legal constraints to pay employee pensions.

4 Agency Funds account for money collected for another entity. An example would be a county which collects property taxes for local school districts. The county is an agent for the school districts and would retain money collected in an Agency Fund until it is distributed to the school districts.

Number of Funds A state or local government should have only one General Fund. It may use as many funds of the other fund types as are needed to account for the different projects, activities, or specially designated purposes that are part of the government operations. However, the GASB recommends using a minimum number of funds.

Account Groups In addition to funds, governments use accounting entities known as **account groups** to maintain records of certain assets and liabilities. These groups are accounting entities, but they are not fiscal entities since they do not control financial resources. Account groups are created to maintain records of fixed assets acquired from general government revenues and long-term liabilities to be paid out of these revenues. Governmental funds have a spending measurement focus. They record only the current budgetary year since they exist to record fiscal year revenues and expenditures. Long-term assets and long-term liabilities, on the other hand, normally are not recorded in these funds since they do not represent expendable resources. Therefore, account groups are established to maintain information about long-term assets and long-term liabilities as a basis for presentation in the financial reports. The two types of account groups are discussed below.

The General Fixed Assets Account Group The general fixed assets account group is used to maintain a record of fixed assets purchased with revenues accounted for in the governmental funds. Transactions involving acquisition or disposal of general government buildings, machinery, or equipment would affect the fixed assets reported in the general fixed assets account group. Fixed assets purchased by proprietary funds are recorded by those funds and are not part of the general fixed assets group. The general fixed asset account group also maintains a summary of the sources of the money expended to acquire the assets (for example, general fund revenues). Depreciation is not recorded for assets in this account group.

The General Long-Term Debt Account Group The general long-term debt account group is used to maintain a record of long-term obligations that are to be repaid out of general government revenues. Debt such as general-obligation bonds which pledge the "full-faith and credit" of the government are recorded in this fund. In addition, the noncurrent portion of liabilities resulting from compensated employee absences (such as vacation or sick leave), contingencies, and claims against the government may be recorded in this fund, as should unfunded pension liabilities and other liabilities resulting from postretirement employee benefits. Long-term liabilities of proprietary funds that are to be repaid by those funds are recorded by the proprietary funds and are not included in the general long-term debt group. This account group also identifies the amount of money needed to retire the liabilities in the account group. However, no money is actually accounted for in the group.

Fund Accounting for Nonprofit Organizations Other than Governments

Nonprofit organizations other than governments often account for their resources in a manner similar to that of governments. Some of these nonprofit organizations may be under the control of a governmental unit. State and municipal hospitals and colleges are divisions of a state or local government, as are publicly owned utilities. Since these organizations may be large and have their own managements, they frequently issue financial reports which are separate from those of the sponsoring governmental unit. Depending upon the primary goal of the organization, accounting for these nonprofit organizations may be similar to accounting for businesses that provide similar services. Thus, nonprofit and for-profit hospitals, public and private colleges, and publicly owned and privately owned utilities may follow similar accounting practices.

In the case of nonprofit organizations which sell goods and services to consumers, prices normally are set at a level sufficient to cover a portion or all of the costs of providing the services according to public policy objectives. In the case of business enterprises, the organizations attempt to earn a satisfactory rate of return for their investors. Regardless of whether these organizations are business or nonprofit, they generally provide separable goods and services at a fee to users. In the nonprofit case, however, the fee will not necessarily recover the entire cost of the service but may be subsidized from some other source. Thus, competitive market conditions may not exist for the nonprofit organization's services. Accordingly, accounting and reporting objectives and practices of these organizations are similar to those of governmental units.

The accounting for nonprofit organizations other than governments is unique in certain respects; yet in many ways it is very similar to governmental accounting. Exhibit 2-1 summarizes the types of funds used in the major categories of nonprofit organizations. General operating expenses are paid out of the general fund or the **current unrestricted fund.** Specific-purpose or specially designated items are accounted for in the special revenue or **restricted funds.**

Money placed in trust funds in governments would be placed in **endowment funds** in other nonprofit organizations. The principal (amount that is to be invested) would remain intact within the endowment fund and the earnings would be transferred to either the current restricted or unrestricted funds for expenditure, depending on whether the provider (or donor) restricts the use of the earnings. Agency funds are also called **custodial funds** in some organizations.

Plant funds are used to account for funds to be used for plant replacement and expansion and, in some cases, for fixed assets, capital projects, and debt service. Colleges and universities have the most detailed accounting for plant funds with four subcategories which include unexpended monies, renewal and replacement projects, debt service, and assets–investment in plant.

Unique features of nonprofit accounting do exist for different kinds of organizations. Colleges and universities often have **loan funds** to account for loans to students, faculty, and staff for which there is no parallel in governmental accounting.

EXHIBIT 2-1

TYPES AND PURPOSES OF FUNDS USED BY NONPROFIT ORGANIZATIONS

Fund type	Purpose
State and Local Governments	
Governmental funds:	
General Fund	Current unrestricted operations
Special Revenue Funds	Activities financed with restricted revenues
Capital Projects Funds	Resources used in construction of fixed assets using general revenues and other financing sources
Debt Service Fund	Resources used to repay principal and interest on general long-term debt
Proprietary funds:	
Enterprise Funds	Activities financed by charges to external users
Internal Service Funds	Activities financed by charges to other government departments
Trust and Agency Funds	Resources held or managed on behalf of other governments, employees, or others
Account groups:	
General fixed asset group	Identification of fixed assets acquired with general revenues
General long-term debt group	Identification of principal of long-term debt to be repaid from general revenues
Hospitals	
Unrestricted fund	Resources which can be used to finance general operations
Restricted funds:	
Special-purpose fund	Resources restricted to externally designated operating purposes
Plant replacement and expansion fund	Resources restricted to financing plant replacement and expansion
Endowment fund	Resources restricted to financing activities from investment earnings
Colleges and Universities	
Current funds:	
Unrestricted fund	Resources which can be used to finance general operations
Restricted fund	Resources restricted to externally designated operating purposes
Loan fund	Resources restricted to providing loans
Endowment fund	Resources restricted to financing activities from investment earnings
Annuity and life income fund	Resources which can be used only after specified amounts have been paid to donor or designee
Plant fund	Resources restricted to financing plant replacement and expansion
Agency fund	Resources held on behalf of other parties
Other Nonprofit Organizations	

Similar to colleges and universities except that annuity and life income funds, loan funds, and agency funds normally are not used. The plant fund generally is referred to as the land, building, and equipment fund.

BASIS OF ACCOUNTING FOR FUNDS

In addition to accounting for their operations in a number of accounting entities (funds and groups), governmental and nonprofit organizations differ from businesses with respect to the timing of the recognition of revenues and expenditures or expenses and with respect to what is measured by the accounting system. The **basis of accounting** is the set of rules that determines *when* revenues and expenditures or expenses are recognized. Examples of the basis of accounting include the cash and accrual bases. The **measurement focus** determines **what** is being measured. Different types of measurement focus include the total-resources concept and the all-financial-resources concept. Businesses and certain nonprofit organizations use the total-resources concept that involves recording expenses for the expiration of all assets, including fixed assets. Governmental funds focus on financial resources. Expenditures are recorded when financial resources are consumed. Expenses for the consumption of fixed resources are not recorded.

While some nonprofit organizations (for example, hospitals) use the **accrual basis** of accounting to measure changes in *total resources* similar to businesses, others use the accrual basis for certain funds and a modification of the accrual basis for others. In addition, financial statements of these organizations may measure the change in **financial resources** rather than the change in total resources. This is particularly true of governments.

Modified Accrual Accounting

State and local governments traditionally have used the modified accrual basis of accounting for recording most revenues and expenditures. The **modified accrual** basis of accounting has features of both accrual accounting and cash accounting. For example, revenues are recorded as received in cash except for revenues that are measurable and available. Available means collectible within the current period or soon enough thereafter to be used to pay liabilities of the current period. For example, property taxes levied during the current fiscal period may be recognized as revenue in the current fiscal period if there is reasonable assurance that they will be collected within a short period after year-end.[2] Other revenues that generally are recorded on a modified accrual basis include regularly billed charges, grants, interfund transfers, and income taxes for which taxpayer liability has been established, collectibility is assured, and losses can be estimated reasonably. The modified accrual basis of accounting has been used as the standard measurement basis for governmental funds. Expendable trust and agency funds also have used the modified accrual basis. Proprietary and nonexpendable trust and pension trust funds use the accrual basis.

[2]The GASB *Codification,* Section P70, specifies the period as 60 days.

The timing of expenditure recognition under the modified accrual basis is similar to accrual accounting; expenditures generally are accrued when the related liability is incurred. However, major exceptions are accounting for fixed assets and principal and interest on long-term debt. Amounts paid for the purchase of fixed assets are recorded as expenditures when the assets are purchased. Depreciation normally is not recorded on these assets. Principal and interest on long-term debt are not accrued until legally due since they are not claims against the current period tax revenues. Prepaid expenses traditionally have not been allocated between periods but are recorded as expenditures of the period when paid. Inventory items (for example, supplies) may be expended either when used or at purchase.

Flow of Financial Resources Accounting

Recently, the GASB has adopted changes in the measurement focus of governmental fund accounting.[3] The **flow of financial resources measurement focus** will become the standard for financial reporting by governmental funds for fiscal periods beginning after June 15, 1994. Under this focus, the effects of transactions are recognized when an increase or decrease in net financial resources occurs, regardless of when cash is received. **Financial resources** include cash, current receivables, and prepaid expenses.

Under this measurement focus the accrual basis of accounting is applied to events that result in changes in financial resources. Revenues from taxes, fines, and donations should be recognized in the period in which the event that increases financial resources takes place, rather than in the period in which cash is received. Therefore, taxes are recorded in the period in which they are demanded or are owed to the government. Sales and income taxes are revenues of the period in which the sales occurred or the income was earned by the taxpayer, subject to the practical limitations of determining the amount owed to the government. Revenues from the sale of goods or services, such as user fees, are recognized when the sale occurs.

Expenditures are recognized under the flow of financial resources focus when the exchanges that create the expenditures occur, not necessarily when cash is paid. Expenditures for fixed assets are recorded when the assets are acquired. Debt service expenditures are recognized when they are due. Prepaid items will be recorded as financial resources when paid for and as expenditures when the underlying service is consumed.

Debt that is issued to fund the operations of the general government, rather than to purchase fixed assets, and that is to be repaid from general fund revenues should not be reported as an other financing source. Interest expendi-

---

[3]*Governmental Accounting Standards Board Statement No. 11,* "Measurement Focus and Basis of Accounting—Governmental Fund Operating Statements," May 1990.

tures should be recognized on this debt as it accrues. Repayment of operating debt principal should not be reported as an other financing use.

The flow of financial resources focus attempts to identify revenues and expenditures with the fiscal period in which the events that gave rise to the revenues and expenditures occurred. This measurement process is consistent with the **intergenerational equity concept,** also referred to as the **interperiod equity concept.**[4] Under this concept, each fiscal period should be accountable for the resources used to provide benefits during that period. In other words, the burden of providing current services should not be shifted to future periods or generations of taxpayers. Therefore, revenues and expenditures should be recognized in the period in which the underlying transactions that gave rise to the revenues and expenditures occurred, not necessarily in the period in which the cash was received or paid.

Proposed GASB accounting standards indicate a trend toward accrual of substantial unrecorded liabilities such as unfunded pensions, leases, uninsured risk, and contingent liabilities. Considerable variation exists in practice in the application of the criteria for measurement of revenues and expenditures by governments. Use of accrual accounting is recommended whenever possible.

GOVERNMENT FINANCIAL REPORTING MODEL

While the financial reports of some nonprofit organizations, such as hospitals, appear similar to those of business organizations, the reports of other governmental and nonprofit organizations are much more extensive than those of most businesses. This is especially true of state and local governments. The financial reports of these governments often contain an extensive number of financial statements, describing various funds and fund types.

As discussed earlier in this chapter, governments may provide both comprehensive and general-purpose financial reports. The **financial reporting pyramid** (described in Exhibit 2-2) provides for the following accounting reports and related information listed in order of the degree of summarization:

1 Condensed summary data
2 General-purpose financial statements (GPFS)
3 Combining statements by fund type
4 Individual fund and account group statements
5 Schedules
6 Transaction data (the accounting system)

We can see from Exhibit 2-2 that reporting builds from the bottom of the pyramid, that is, the accounting system in which all transactions are recorded, to a condensed summary with minimal detail at the top of the pyramid. The

[4]GASB *Codification*, Sections 100.603–100.608.

EXHIBIT 2-2
THE FINANCIAL REPORTING PYRAMID

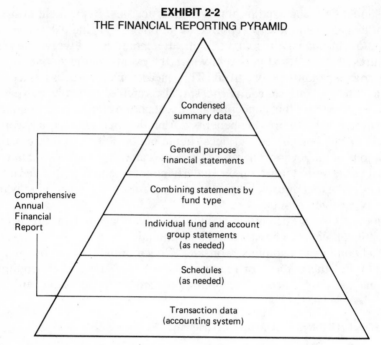

Source: GASB *Codification,* Section 1900.114.

comprehensive annual financial report consists of items 2 (GPFS) through 5 (schedules, as needed). **Combined statements** provide a summarization of all of the major fund types and account groups. A column is provided for each fund type (General, Special Revenue, Capital Projects, etc.). **Combining statements** summarize the accounts for all funds of the same type; for example, account totals for all special revenue funds would be reported. The CAFR should be prepared in conformance with generally accepted accounting principles (GAAP). A CAFR consists of the following statements:[5]

1 Statements of financial position:
   a Combined balance sheet for all fund types and account groups.
   b Combining balance sheets for all funds of each type.
   c Individual balance sheets for each fund and account group as necessary to fairly present the financial position of each fund and account group and any schedules necessary to demonstrate legal and/or contractual compliance.
2 Operating statements:
   a Governmental funds:

[5]GASB *Codification,* Sections 1900.112–1900.113.

    (1) Combined statement of revenues, expenditures, and changes in fund balance.

    (2) Combined statement of revenues, expenditures, and changes in fund balance (budget compared with actual) for general and special revenue funds as well as other funds with legally adopted budgets.

    (3) Combining statement of revenues, expenditures, and changes in fund balance by fund type.

    (4) Individual statements of revenues, expenditures, and changes in fund balance for each fund when necessary and any schedules necessary to demonstrate legal and/or contractual compliance.

b Proprietary funds:

    (1) Combined statement of revenues, expenses, and changes in retained earnings.

    (2) Combined statement of cash flows.

    (3) Combining statement of revenues and expenses by fund type.

    (4) Combining statement of cash flows by fund type.

    (5) Individual statements of revenue and expenses and statements of cash flow by fund where necessary and any schedules necessary to demonstrate legal or financial compliance.

c Fiduciary funds:

    (1) Expendable trust funds should include statements as listed above under **a** for governmental funds.

    (2) Nonexpendable trust funds should include statements as listed above under **b** for proprietary funds.

    (3) At the combined statements–overview level, trust funds may be presented separately or within the governmental and proprietary fund types.

    (4) Combining statement of changes in assets and liabilities for all agency funds.

d Account groups:

    (1) Statement of changes in general fixed assets.

    (2) Statement of changes in general long-term debt.

    (3) Either **(1)** or **(2)** may be eliminated if sufficient note disclosure is made.

THE STATEMENT OF FINANCIAL POSITION

This section describes the statement of financial position or balance sheet for various types of governmental and nonprofit organizations. We first will discuss the statement presentation for state and local governments and then discuss the presentation for other types of nonprofit organizations.

Balance Sheets for Governmental Units

Exhibit 2-3 provides an example of a *combined balance sheet* for the City of East River. This balance sheet contains separate columns for nine accounting entities including seven fund types and two account groups. This combined

EXHIBIT 2-3
CITY OF EAST RIVER
COMBINED BALANCE SHEET—ALL FUNDS AND ACCOUNT GROUPS
DECEMBER 31, 19X1
($ IN THOUSANDS)

	Governmental funds				Proprietary funds		Fiduciary funds	Account groups		Totals (memorandum only)	
	General	Special revenue	Debt service	Capital projects	Enterprise	Internal service	Trust and agency	General fixed assets	Long-term debt	December 31, 19X1	December 31, 19X0
Assets											
Cash	$305	$100	$ 40	$ 430	$ 250	$ 30	$ 210			$ 1,365	$ 1,250
Investments, at cost	70	40	272				1,200			1,582	2,000
Receivables, net:											
Taxes	60	3			29		580			643	710
Accounts	10	4								43	33
Due from other funds	2				2	12	10			26	18
Due from other governments	30	75		640						745	101
Inventory of supplies	8	5			23	40				76	70
Land					210	20		$1,300		1,530	1,460
Buildings					445	60		2,900		3,405	2,840
Accumulated depreciation					(90)	(5)				(95)	(84)
Improvements other than buildings					3,800	15		1,000		4,815	3,920
Accumulated depreciation					(400)	(3)				(403)	(284)
Machinery and equipment					1,800	25		450		2,275	1,924
Accumulated depreciation					(200)	(10)				(210)	(142)
Construction in progress					23			1,700		1,723	1,360
Amount available in debt service fund									$ 210	210	285
Amount to be provided for retirement of general long-term debt									1,900	1,900	1,075
Total assets	$485	$227	$312	$1,070	$5,892	$184	$2,000	$7,350	$2,110	$19,630	$16,536

42

Liabilities and Fund Equity

Liabilities

Vouchers payable	$118	$34		$29	$131	$15	$3			$ 330	$ 223
Contracts payable	58	18		69	8					153	330
Accrued interest					32					32	67
Revenue bonds payable					48					48	52
Due to other taxing units							690			690	200
Due to other funds	24	2		1						27	17
Matured bonds payable			$100							100	
Matured interest payable			2							2	
General obligation bonds					700				$2,110	2,810	2,640
Total liabilities	$200	$54	$102	$ 99	$ 919	$15	$ 693	$ 0	$2,110	$ 4,192	$ 3,529
Fund equity:											
Contributed capital					$1,400	$77				$ 1,477	$ 815
Investments in general fixed assets								$7,350		7,350	5,300
Retained earnings:											
Reserved for revenue bond retirement					130					130	97
Unreserved					1,914	74				1,988	3,434
Fund balances:											
Reserved for encumbrances	$ 38	$ 47		$ 940						1,025	1,410
Reserved for inventory of supplies	8	5								13	11
Reserved for employee retirement system							958			958	1,415
Unreserved:											
Designated for debt service			$210							210	325
Undesignated	239	121		31	1,529	18	349			2,287	200
Total fund equity	$285	$173	$210	$ 971	$4,973	$169	$1,307	$7,350	$ 0	$15,438	$13,007
Total liabilities and fund equity	$485	$227	$312	$1,070	$5,892	$184	$2,000	$7,350	$2,110	$19,630	$16,536

balance sheet is required as a component part of both the comprehensive annual financial report and the general-purpose financial statements of governments. The Total column includes the sum of all of the other columns for each account. Transactions between funds (for example, short-term loans from the general fund to a special revenue fund) normally are not eliminated in preparing the Total column. Interfund eliminations are not considered to be appropriate since each fund is a legally separate accounting and fiscal entity.

Assets included on the balance sheet for most fund types are similar to those of business organizations. The governmental and fiduciary funds report current assets (cash, short-term investments, receivables, and prepaid items such as supplies). Fixed assets are reported in addition to current assets by proprietary funds. Accumulated depreciation is reported for proprietary fund assets. The fixed assets purchased with general revenues are reported in the general fixed asset account group. Accumulated depreciation is not recorded for these assets in the governmental funds. Accumulated depreciation may be reported in the general fixed asset account group but seldom is in practice. *Construction in Progress* is the total cost incurred for capital projects that are not yet completed. The Asset section of the general long-term debt account group includes two accounts: *Amount Available in Debt Service Fund* for payment of debt principal and *Amount to be Provided for Retirement of General Long-Term Debt*. The "amount available" represents financial resources that have been set aside in the debt service fund to pay the principal of currently maturing debt. The debt service fund also may report financial resources available for payment of interest. Therefore, the magnitude of the assets of the debt service fund may be larger than the amount available reported by the general long-term debt group. The total of the Amount Available and "Amount to Be Provided" accounts should be equal to the amount of long-term debt reported in this account group.

The liabilities of governmental units are similar to those of businesses. Long-term liabilities are not reported by governmental funds. These liabilities are reported in the general long-term debt account group. The amount of principal and interest to be paid during the current period from general revenues is reported in the debt service fund. Traditionally, interest has not been accrued on this debt for the period between the last interest payment date before the fiscal year-end and the end of the fiscal year since the interest will be paid out of next year's revenues. However, this interest is accruable under recent guidelines from the GASB if a legal obligation arises during the current fiscal year. Interest is accrued by the enterprise funds on debt to be repaid out of enterprise revenues.

Since there are no direct owners of a government, in the sense of a business enterprise, who have the right to buy and sell ownership shares, the Owners' Equity section of the balance sheet is replaced with **fund balance** accounts for governmental and fiduciary funds. These accounts report the excess of fund assets over fund liabilities and any restrictions on the excess that would indicate that the fund balance may not be used in the future. For example, a re-

serve for supplies indicates that a portion of the assets represented by the fund balance has already been used to purchase supplies and will not be available for other service requirements. Further, a **reserve for encumbrances** indicates that a portion of the resources will be needed in the future to pay for goods that have been ordered but have not yet been received during the current period.

The **fund equity** accounts report the excess of assets over liabilities for the proprietary funds. *Contributed capital* represents the amount transferred permanently from the general government to the enterprise funds to establish them as operating entities. Retained earnings are accumulated for proprietary funds as they are for corporations.

Investment in general fixed assets indicates the total cost of all fixed assets reported in the general fixed asset account group.

Since funds are considered to be separate accounting entities, assets and liabilities are sometimes double counted in combined balance sheets. For example, assets currently available in the debt service fund for principal repayment may be shown also in the asset section of the general long-term debt account group. As discussed above, amounts due from one fund to another are not eliminated as is the case in business reporting. The Total column of the combined balance sheet (in Exhibit 2-3) does not eliminate this double counting; and further, it may present numbers created from two different bases of accounting: modified accrual and accrual. Consequently, assets and liabilities are frequently overstated in the Total column. Therefore, care must be used in interpreting the data in this column and it should be marked "Memorandum Only." In this type of report, attention should be focused on the individual funds rather than on the combined totals.

A government may have more than one special revenue, debt service, capital projects, enterprise, internal service, trust, or agency fund. Exhibit 2-4 describes a balance sheet that reports separate assets and equities for each of the funds of a specific type. This balance sheet is a combining balance sheet in that it combines the funds from a given type of fund. A government's comprehensive annual financial report should include a combining statement for all funds of a specific type. The Total column from the combining statement (Exhibit 2-4) should correspond with the respective column for that type of fund in the combined balance sheet (Exhibit 2-3). Separate balance sheets may be provided for individual funds when only one fund of a given type exists or when additional detail is needed that is not part of the combined or combining statements.

Other Nonprofit Balance Sheets

Exhibit 2-5 presents a fund-based balance sheet of a hypothetical hospital organized as a nonprofit entity. Two primary groups of funds are shown—unrestricted and restricted. The *unrestricted fund* controls resources intended for general operating purposes. Resources that have been restricted by manage-

EXHIBIT 2-4
CITY OF EAST RIVER
COMBINING BALANCE SHEET—ALL SPECIAL REVENUE FUNDS
DECEMBER 31, 19X1
($ IN THOUSANDS)

	Parks	State gasoline tax	Motor vehicle license	Parking	Totals	
					December 31, 19X1	December 31, 19X0
Assets						
Cash	$40	$22	$ 5	$33	$100	$ 91
Investments, at cost	16			24	40	25
Receivables, net:						
Taxes	3				3	
Accounts	4				4	3
Due from state		47	28		75	62
Inventory of supplies	1	1	1	2	5	5
Total assets	$64	$70	$34	$59	$227	$186
Liabilities and Fund Balances						
Liabilities:						
Vouchers payable	$10	$11	$ 4	$ 9	$ 34	$ 23
Contracts payable	13	4		1	18	12
Due to general fund	2				2	
Total liabilities	$25	$15	$ 4	$10	$ 54	$ 35
Fund balances:						
Reserved for encumbrances	$14	$17	$10	$ 6	$ 47	$ 13
Reserved for inventory of supplies	1	1	1	2	5	5
Unreserved	24	37	19	41	121	133
Total fund balances	$39	$55	$30	$49	$173	$151
Total liabilities and fund balances	$64	$70	$34	$59	$227	$186

ment (rather than by external providers) for specific purposes should be included in this fund as "board-designated assets." Only resources that are restricted by external limitations imposed by donors or creditors are included in *restricted funds*. The distinction between unrestricted and restricted is one of control and management discretion. If management can restrict the resources at their own discretion, the resources are treated as unrestricted for accounting purposes. Most nonprofit hospitals have a capital maintenance objective in which the cost of fixed assets and debt repayment are intended to be recovered from charges to patients. Accordingly, fixed assets (along with accumulated depreciation) and long-term liabilities are reported as part of the unrestricted fund.

EXHIBIT 2-5
CITY HOSPITAL
BALANCE SHEET
DECEMBER 31, 19X1
($ IN THOUSANDS)

Assets			Liabilities and fund balances		

Unrestricted Fund

Current assets:			Current liabilities:		
Cash....................................		$ 10	Notes payable to banks..............		$ 10
Receivables, net		50	Accounts payable.....................		30
Inventories.............................		17	Accrued expenses payable..........		14
Prepaid expenses.....................		5	Current portion of long-term debt...		8
Total current assets................		$ 82	Deferred revenue		4
Board-designated assets:					
Cash...........................	$ 5		Total current liabilities...........		$ 66
Investments..................	60		Long-term liabilities:		
			Bonds payable..................	$ 60	
Total board-designated assets ...		65	Mortgage payable............	100	
Plant assets:					
Land, buildings, and			Total long-term liabilities........		160
equipment..................	$610				
Less accumulated			Total liabilities....................		$226
depreciation................	300		Fund balance		$231
Net plant assets....................		310			
			Total unrestricted fund liabilities		
Total unrestricted fund assets		$457	and fund balance......................		$457

Restricted Funds
Specific-Purpose Fund

Cash......................................		$ 10	Liabilities..................................		$ 5
Investments		85	Fund balance		90
			Total specific-purpose fund		
Total specific-purpose fund assets....		$ 95	liabilities and fund balance		$ 95

Plant Replacement and Expansion Fund

Cash......................................		$ 20			
Investments		170			
Total plant replacement and					
expansion fund assets		$190	Fund balance		$190

Endowment Fund

Cash......................................		$ 30			
Investments		280			
Total endowment fund assets..........		$310	Fund balance		$310

Restricted funds may be separated into specific-purpose, plant replacement and expansion, and endowment funds. **Specific-purpose funds** are similar to special revenue funds of governments. These funds consist primarily of monetary resources that are restricted by donors or grantors for specific purposes other than the acquisition of fixed assets. Monetary resources that are restricted for the acquisition of fixed assets are controlled by **plant replacement and expansion funds.** As the resources in these funds are used to acquire fixed assets or are otherwise consumed as intended by the donor, they are transferred out of the restricted funds. Acquired assets are recorded in the unrestricted fund. Thus, plant replacement and expansion funds exist on a temporary basis until their functions are completed.

Endowment funds report resources donated to a hospital that are to be invested. The principal in an endowment fund is not expendable, and only earnings on the investments may be used to support current activities. The earnings should be transferred to the unrestricted fund and are not part of the endowment fund unless they are intended to increase the amount of the endowment.

Other types of nonprofit organizations also may use fund-based balance sheets. Colleges and universities use **current funds** to account for monetary resources used in current operations. These funds are divided into unrestricted and restricted funds in a manner similar to general and special revenue funds of governments. Other funds include **loan funds** to account for money available for loans and for receivables from loans; *endowment funds*; **annuity and life income funds** for resources that must be held in trust for a certain period during the life of the donor or recipient of income from the resources; *plant funds* for resources held for plant acquisition and replacement, for repayment of debt, and for fixed assets; and **agency funds.** Similar funds frequently are maintained by other health, welfare, and public service organizations. These organizations frequently use current unrestricted and restricted funds, plant funds, endowment funds, agency funds, and loan funds.

The FASB and AICPA recently have considered a variety of financial reporting issues for nonprofit organizations. Some organizations are abandoning the traditional fund-based reporting format in favor of a single-column format in which all funds are aggregated into one set of numbers. Financial reporting by nonprofit organizations currently is in transition, and a variety of formats may be observed in practice.

Summary of Balance Sheet Reporting

In summary, the following key points should be noted:

1 Balance sheets for governmental and nonprofit organizations contain similar information to that contained in business balance sheets—resources, obligations, and residual claims.

2 Governmental and nonprofit balance sheets are normally presented for separate accounting entities known as funds and account groups.

3 Different funds and groups may report different types of assets and liabilities. Some may report only current items. Others may report only long-term items.

4 Fund balance replaces owners' equity on governmental and nonprofit balance sheets. Fund balance reserves represent resources that have been committed for a specific use and are not available for expenditure for other purposes.

OPERATING STATEMENTS

This section describes the operating statements for various governmental and nonprofit organizations. Statements of operating results for state and local governments are discussed first, followed by a discussion for other nonprofit organizations.

Statements of Operating Results for Governments

As discussed earlier, the primary operating activities of a governmental unit are not intended to earn a profit or return for investors. Revenues generally are not earned by the direct sale of goods and services. Rather, most revenues are generated by taxes received from taxing residents of a specific geographic area. The cost of providing goods and services must be paid from revenues, but these costs cannot be matched with sales since most services are not sold directly to consumers. Since there is no direct relationship between the cost incurred in producing goods and services and the revenue produced from selling these products, a profit-oriented income statement is not reported for most funds.

Instead, a statement of revenues, expenditures, and changes in fund balance should be provided to report the activities of governmental and expendable trust funds. A combined statement is illustrated in Exhibit 2-6.

Governmental funds and expendable trust funds account for only financial resources, that is, monetary resources and those resources (prepaid items) that are expected to be consumed during the current operating period. The operating statement is intended to demonstrate that these financial resources were expended during the current fiscal year to provide services to taxpayers in accordance with an approved budget. Thus, no attempt is made to allocate some portion of the cost of fixed assets to the current period through depreciation as would be appropriate under a capital maintenance–net income approach to measurement.

Also, most revenues and expenses that do not result in or require the use of expendable resources in the current period are not accrued. Governmental funds use the modified accrual basis. Revenues are recorded when they are

EXHIBIT 2-6
CITY OF EAST RIVER
COMBINED STATEMENT OF REVENUES, EXPENDITURES, AND CHANGES IN FUND BALANCES—ALL GOVERNMENTAL FUND TYPES AND EXPENDABLE TRUST FUNDS FOR THE FISCAL YEAR ENDED DECEMBER 31, 19X1
($ IN THOUSANDS)

| | Governmental fund types | | | | Fiduciary fund type | Totals (memorandum only) year ended | |
	General	Special revenue	Debt service	Capital projects	Expendable Trust	December 31, 19X1	December 31, 19X0
Revenues:							
Taxes	$ 881	$ 189	$ 79			$1,149	$1,138
Licenses and permits	103					103	97
Intergovernmental revenues	187	831	42	$1,250		2,310	1,509
Charges for services	91	79				170	160
Fines and forfeits	33					33	26
Miscellaneous revenues	20	72	7	4		103	112
Total revenues	$1,315	$1,171	$128	$1,254		$3,868	$3,042
Expenditures:							
Current:							
General government	$ 122					$ 122	$ 134
Public safety	258	$ 480				738	671
Highways and streets	85	417				502	409
Sanitation	56					56	44

Health	45					45	37
Welfare	47					47	41
Recreation	41	256				297	286
Education	509				2	511	512
Capital outlay				$1,626		1,626	803
Debt service:							
Principal retirement			$ 60			60	52
Interest and fiscal charges			40			40	50
Total expenditures	$1,163	$1,153	$100	$1,626	$2	$4,044	$3,039
Excess of revenues over (under) expenditures	$ 152	$ 18	$ 28	$ (372)	$ (2)	$ (176)	$ 3
Other financing sources (uses):							
Proceeds of general obligation bonds				$ 900		$ 900	
Operating transfers in				65	$ 2	67	$ 89
Operating transfers out	$ (75)					(75)	(87)
Total other financing sources (uses)	$ (75)			$ 965	$ 2	$ 892	$ 2
Excess of revenues and other sources over (under) expenditures and other uses	$ 77	$ 18	$ 28	$ 593		$ 716	$ 5
Fund balances—January 1	208	155	182	378	$27	711	1,207
Fund balances—December 31	$ 285	$ 173	$ 210	$ 971	$27	$1,427	$1,212

available and measurable and expenditures are recognized when measurable liabilities are incurred that are expected to be paid out of revenues generated in the current operating period. Governmental operating statements report revenues *by source.*

An **expenditure** refers to the use of monetary resources, whereas an **expense** refers to the expiration of monetary or nonmonetary resources in the production of revenue in a profit-oriented system. Governmental fund operating statements report expenditures *by function.* The function indicates the nature of the service activity that was provided by use of the resources. Expenditures for fixed assets and to pay principal and interest on long-term debt are reported by the funds which are responsible for the expenditures.

Governmental fund operating statements present the inflow and outflow of financial resources, while business statements match expenses with the revenues they produce. In addition, business reports are concerned with depicting operating events over time on a going-concern basis. Long-run profitability, profit potential, and risk associated with future earnings are major concerns of investors. Government reports are concerned with demonstrating that resources acquired in the current period were utilized to meet current service requirements in the current operating period, consistent with the intergenerational equity concept. The ability of a governmental unit to provide services beyond the current fiscal period is not a primary focus of operating statements under contemporary reporting practices.

The difference between governmental funds and business enterprises is readily seen in accounting for fixed assets. Governmental funds record an expenditure for a fixed asset when it is purchased and when monetary resources are consumed. The asset is then recorded as an increase in the general fixed asset group. No depreciation is recorded during the life of such an asset since future monetary resources will not be consumed by use of the asset and capital maintenance is not a measurement purpose of governmental reporting. However, businesses record the purchase as an asset. A portion of the asset cost is expensed each period as the asset is consumed in producing goods and services to be sold during the current period as part of the capital maintenance approach to net income measurement.

Other differences between businesses and governmental operations are observable in accounting for long-term debt. The proceeds of debt issues are reported as part of governmental fund resource inflows (**other financing sources**) since they provide monetary resources that can be consumed during the current period. These resources are separated from revenues since they must be repaid. Subsequently, repayment of the debt is recorded periodically as an expenditure of general fund resources since general fund resources are used to repay the debt.

Another major area of accounting difference involves interfund transfers. A transfer from the general fund to the debt service fund is an outflow of financial resources for the general fund and an inflow for the debt service fund since monetary resources decrease in the general fund and increase in the debt service fund. However, the total resources of the government have not changed; therefore, these interfund inflows and outflows are separated from other resource flows in the operating statement and are reported as **operating transfers.**

Another area of difference involves outstanding purchase orders. Most funds encumber expendable resources when purchase orders for goods and services to be acquired by fund resources are approved. These **encumbrances** represent planned expenditures but are not legal obligations until title to the goods passes to the government or until services are received. In business accounting, no obligation is recorded when a purchase order is issued since no legal requirement to pay has been created at that point. At the point legal obligations are incurred in a governmental organization, expenditures are recorded. Encumbrances serve to restrict expendable resources to prevent overspending of a specific budget item. However, encumbrances are not expenditures, and encumbrances outstanding at fiscal year-end should not be reported as expenditures on the operating statement.

At the end of an accounting period, the excess of revenues over expenditures is transferred (closed) to the fund balances of the respective funds. These excesses can be used to reduce future resource needs or to offset future deficits in the event that expenditures are larger than revenues in those periods. The end-of-year fund balance reported on the operating statement should correspond with the fund balance reported on the balance sheet of the respective funds (see Exhibit 2-4).

General-purpose financial statements of governmental units contain only the combined operating statements. In addition to the combined statements, the comprehensive annual financial report of a government contains combining statements of revenues, expenditures, and changes in fund balances for each fund type with more than one separate fund. A combining statement for special revenue funds is shown in Exhibit 2-7. The Total column of these statements corresponds to the respective column for the fund type in the combined statement (see Exhibit 2-6).

Proprietary funds and certain trust funds of governments operate in a manner similar to businesses since they provide separable products for which a sales price can be determined. Frequently the organizations for which such fund accounting systems are maintained have capital maintenance objectives. In these situations, goods and services are provided to consumers who are charged a price for those goods and services. Accordingly, operating statements for these funds should be similar to those of businesses that employ a capital maintenance approach to measurement. Exhibit 2-8 illustrates a combined statement of revenues, expenses, and changes in retained earnings/fund balances for such funds.

Since capital maintenance and net income are the primary focuses of such systems, the accrual basis of accounting is used for these funds. Expenses rather than expenditures are recorded since they represent the cost of producing revenue. Depreciation of fixed assets is recorded as an expense in such systems. The proceeds of debt issues are not recorded in the operating state-

EXHIBIT 2-7
CITY OF EAST RIVER
COMBINING STATEMENT OF REVENUES, EXPENDITURES, AND CHANGES IN FUND
BALANCES—ALL SPECIAL REVENUE FUNDS
FOR THE FISCAL YEAR ENDED DECEMBER 31, 19X1
($ IN THOUSANDS)

| | | State gasoline tax | Motor vehicle license | | Totals year ended | |
	Parks			Parking	December 31, 19X1	December 31, 19X0
Revenues:						
Taxes	$189				$ 189	$168
Intergovernmental revenues		$630	$201		831	550
Charges for services				$79	79	71
Miscellaneous revenues	72				72	64
Total revenues	$261	$630	$201	$79	$1,171	$853
Expenditures:						
Public safety		$199	$200	$81	$ 480	$214
Highways and streets		417			417	346
Recreation	$256				256	238
Total expenditures	$256	$616	$200	$81	$1,153	$798
Excess of revenues over (under) expenditures	$ 5	$ 14	$ 1	$ (2)	$ 18	$ 55
Fund balances—January 1	48	50	28	29	155	100
Fund balances—December 31	$ 53	$ 64	$ 29	$27	$ 173	$155

ment as resource inflows nor is the repayment of debt principal treated as an operating transaction. Transfers between these funds and other funds are usually reported in the operating statement; however, these amounts are separated from other sources and uses of fund resources.

As was true of governmental funds, combining statements for proprietary and fiduciary fund types, when more than one fund of the same type exist, are provided in the comprehensive annual financial report. The Total column from the combining statements corresponds to the respective column in the combined statement.

Operating Statements for Nonprofit Organizations Other than Governments

Operating statements of some nonprofit organizations are generally similar to those of businesses since these organizations normally generate a major portion of their revenues by selling goods and services to their customers or members and their organizations have a capital maintenance objective. Exhibit 2-9 shows the income statement of a hospital in which the accrual basis of ac-

EXHIBIT 2-8
CITY OF EAST RIVER
COMBINED STATEMENT OF REVENUES, EXPENSES, AND CHANGES IN RETAINED
EARNINGS/FUND BALANCES—ALL PROPRIETARY FUND TYPES AND SIMILAR
TRUST FUNDS
FOR THE FISCAL YEAR ENDED DECEMBER 31, 19X1
($ IN THOUSANDS)

	Enter-prise	Internal service	Non-expend-able trust	Pension trust	December 31, 19X1	December 31, 19X0
Operating revenues:						
Charges for services	$ 672	$ 88			$ 760	$ 687
Interest			$ 2	$ 28	30	26
Contributions				161	161	145
Gifts			45		45	
Total operating revenues	$ 672	$ 88	$ 47	$189	$ 996	$ 858
Operating expenses:						
Personal services	$ 247	$ 32			$ 279	$ 250
Contractual services	75				75	68
Supplies	20	1			21	17
Materials	51	44			95	88
Utilities	26	1			27	23
Depreciation	144	4			148	133
Benefit payments				$ 21	21	12
				26	26	13
Total operating expenses	$ 563	$ 82		$ 47	$ 692	$ 604
Operating income	$ 109	$ 6	$ 47	$142	$ 304	$ 254
Nonoperating revenues (expenses):						
Operating grants	$ 55				$ 55	$ 50
Interest revenue	4				4	3
Rent	5				5	5
Interest expense and fiscal charges	(93)				(93)	(102)
Total nonoperating revenues (expenses)	$ (29)				$ (29)	$ (44)
Income before operating transfers	$ 80	$ 6	$ 47	$142	$ 275	$ 210
Operating transfers in (out)			(2)		(2)	(3)
Net income	$ 80	$ 6	$ 45	$142	$ 273	$ 207
Retained earnings/fund balances—January 1	4,893	163	140	644	5,840	5,633
Retained earnings/fund balances—December 31	$4,973	$169	$185	$786	$6,113	$5,840

EXHIBIT 2-9
CITY HOSPITAL
INCOME STATEMENT
YEAR ENDED DECEMBER 31, 19X1
($ IN THOUSANDS)

Patient service revenues	$ 400	
Less allowances and uncollectibles	60	
Net patient service revenues		$ 340
Other operating revenues		30
Total operating revenues		$ 370
Less operating expenses:		
Nursing services	$ 110	
Other professional services	80	
General services	100	
Fiscal services	20	
Administrative services (including interest expense of $4)	15	
Provision for depreciation	10	
Total operating expenses		$ 335
Income from operations		$ 35
Nonoperating revenues:		
Unrestricted gifts and bequests	$ 20	
Unrestricted income from endowment fund	10	
Total nonoperating revenues		30
Net income for the year		$ 65

counting is used. It should be noted that expenses, including depreciation, are recorded in such statements.

The revenue-generating activities of a hospital should be reported in the unrestricted fund. The resources of restricted funds may change during a fiscal period but not because of revenue-generating activities. Changes in resources that occur from nonoperating activities are reported in the statement of changes in fund balances for these funds. Exhibit 2-10 reports this information for hospital restricted and unrestricted funds. The emphasis in this statement is on resource flows from donations, purchase and sale of fixed assets, issuance and retirement of debt, and similar items.

Other types of nonprofit organizations can report operations using statements similar to those of governments. For example, colleges and universities provide a statement of current fund revenues and expenditures that is similar to the operating statement of governmental funds. Statements of changes in fund balances are provided for all college funds. Officially, colleges use the accrual basis for revenue and expenditure recognition. However, expenditures not expenses are reported, and depreciation traditionally has not been recorded on fixed assets unless provision is made for their replacement by investments of monetary resources. Certain public service organizations such as churches and museums follow similar reporting practices for operations to those of colleges, including the treatment of expenditures and depreciation.

EXHIBIT 2-10
CITY HOSPITAL
STATEMENT OF CHANGES IN FUND BALANCES
YEAR ENDED DECEMBER 31, 19X1
($ IN THOUSANDS)

Unrestricted Fund

Fund balance, January 1		$158
Net income for the year		65
Transfers from plant replacement and expansion fund for plant asset acquisitions		20
Transfers to plant replacement and expansion fund of third-party reimbursement restricted to plant asset acquisition		(12)
Fund balance, December 31		$231

Restricted Funds

Specific-Purpose Fund

Fund balance, January 1		$ 90
Restricted gifts and bequests received		10
Research grants received		8
Restricted income from investments		5
Gain on sale of investments		2
Transfers to unrestricted fund for:		
Allowances and uncollectable accounts	$ (4)	
Other operating revenue	(16)	(20)
Fund balance, December 31		$ 95

Plant Replacement and Expansion Fund

Fund balance, January 1	$163
Restricted gifts and bequests received	20
Restricted income from investments	14
Transfers to unrestricted fund	(15)
Transfer from unrestricted fund	8
Fund balance, December 31	$190

Endowment Fund

Fund balance, January 1	$253
Restricted gifts and bequests received	45
Gain on sale of investments	12
Fund balance, December 31	$310

Recent FASB guidelines require the recording of depreciation expense for certain nonprofit organizations.[6] This is another area of transition in which a diversity of practices may be observed among nonprofit organizations.

Summary of Reporting of Operations

In summary, the key concepts in this discussion of operating statements are

1 Operating statements of governmental and nonprofit organization funds vary depending on whether or not a primary function of the fund is the maintenance of capital and generation of profit.

[6]*Statement of Financial Accounting Standards No. 93*, "Recognition of Depreciation by Not-for-Profit Organizations," FASB, Stamford, 1987.

2 Funds that account for organizations with a capital maintenance or profit objective normally employ a business approach.

3 Funds that reflect traditional nonprofit goals measure the inflow and out-flow of expendable resources during the current period.

4 Resource flows for governmental and nonprofit funds should be segregated between those that have an effect on total organization net resources and those that do not.

COMPARING BUDGETS TO ACTUAL RESULTS

Some funds, such as governmental funds, are controlled by legally adopted budgets that specify how resources are to be expended and that identify how resources are to be obtained during an operating period. Managers are expected to comply with the budget in obtaining and using resources. In the event that resources are not available to meet the budget requirements or if service demands change so that the budgeted amounts for certain functions are inadequate, formal approval of budget modifications is required.

A primary means of monitoring the activities of government management is to compare actual and budgeted operations. A **statement of revenues, expenditures, and changes in fund balances—budget and actual,** is designed for this purpose as shown in Exhibit 2-11. This statement is required for all funds that are controlled by legally adopted budgets. Certain governmental funds, for example, capital projects and debt service funds, may not have budgets if the amounts of the projects are small or if the fund resources are controlled by external contracts or bond indentures.

Budget and actual comparisons underscore variances between the budget and actual operating results. Small variances are normal since the budget is only an estimate of expected activities. Large variances may be a cause of concern to council, managers, or creditors and may require investigation and modification of operating procedures. In some cases, overexpenditure of authorized budget levels can have serious legal consequences for managers.

Although general-purpose financial statements contain only combined reports, the comprehensive annual financial report of governmental units also should include budget and actual comparisons for all individual funds for which legally adopted budgets are required.

Occasionally, governments use a basis of accounting for budgetary purposes that differs from the basis used for financial reporting. For example, the cash basis may be used for budgets and the modified accrual basis may be used for financial reporting. In such cases the budget and actual comparison should be made on the budget basis, and the actual amounts will probably differ from those reported in other financial statements.

Since most nonprofit organizations other than governments do not adopt legally binding budgets, financial statements comparing budget and actual amounts are not required. However, budgets are important planning and control devices for any organization. Most organizations adopt budgets for these

EXHIBIT 2-11

CITY OF EAST RIVER

COMBINED STATEMENT OF REVENUES, EXPENDITURES, AND CHANGES IN FUND BALANCES—BUDGET AND ACTUAL—GENERAL AND SPECIAL REVENUE FUND TYPES

FOR THE FISCAL YEAR ENDED DECEMBER 31, 19X1

($ IN THOUSANDS)

	General fund			Special revenue funds			Totals (memorandum only)		
	Budget	Actual	Variance (unfavorable)	Budget	Actual	Variance (unfavorable)	Budget	Actual	Variance (unfavorable)
Revenues:									
Taxes	$ 883	$ 881	$ (2)	$ 190	$ 189	$ (1)	$1,073	$1,070	$ (3)
Licenses and permits	126	103	(23)				126	103	(23)
Intergovernmental revenues	200	187	(13)	838	831	(7)	1,038	1,018	(20)
Charges for services	90	91	1	78	79	1	168	170	2
Fines and forfeits	33	33					33	33	
Miscellaneous revenues	20	20		81	72	(9)	101	92	(9)
Total revenues	$1,352	$1,315	$(37)	$1,187	$1,171	$(16)	$2,539	$2,486	$ (53)
Expenditures:									
Current:									
General government	$ 129	$ 122	$ 7				$ 129	$ 122	$ 7
Public safety	277	258	19	$ 495	$ 480	$ 15	772	738	34
Highways and streets	85	85		436	417	19	521	502	19
Sanitation	50	56	(6)				50	56	(6)
Health	48	45	3				48	45	3
Welfare	51	47	4				51	47	4
Culture and recreation	45	41	4	272	256	16	317	297	20
Education	541	509	32				541	509	32
Total expenditures	$1,226	$1,163	$ 63	$1,203	$1,153	$ 50	$2,429	$2,316	$113
Excess of revenues over (under) expenditures	$ 126	$ 152	$ 26	$ (16)	$ 18	$ 34	$ 110	$ 170	$ 60
Other financing sources (uses):									
Operating transfers out	(75)	(75)					(75)	(75)	
Excess of revenues over (under) expenditures and other uses	$ 51	$ 77	$ 26	$ (16)	$ 18	$ 34	$ 35	$ 95	$ 60
Fund balances—January 1	208	208		155	155		363	363	
Fund balances—December 31	$ 259	$ 285	$ 26	$ 139	$ 173	$ 34	$ 398	$ 458	$ 60

purposes. However, they may or may not be legally constrained to follow the budgets and may not be able to control departure from budgeted amounts if revenues decline. Since governmental organizations are not as susceptible to market forces as are other organizations, oversight of the process by which taxes and other revenues are obtained and used in these funds is enhanced by budget and actual comparisons.

THE STATEMENT OF CASH FLOWS

Businesses are required to report a **statement of cash flows** in their annual reports. These statements are intended to explain changes in resources and claims to the resources that are not evident in the income statement. Proprietary and certain fiduciary funds of governments are expected to provide these statements as well, since they operate similarly to businesses.[7] Exhibit 2-12 provides an example of a statement of cash flows for an enterprise fund. The statement emphasizes changes in resources that are not evident from the income statement such as issuance and retirement of debt and purchase and sale of fixed assets. Cash flows are defined as including both cash and cash equivalents. Cash equivalents are short-term, highly liquid investments. The cash flow statement is similar to that of business enterprises with the exception that financing activities are divided into two sections for governmental units: noncapital financing activities and capital financing activities. As in the case of business enterprises, either the direct or the indirect method of preparing the statement of cash flows can be used; however, the GASB encourages the use of the direct method. The total amount of cash reported on the statement of cash flows should be equivalent to the amount of cash reported on the balance sheet for the same fund. The amount of net cash provided by operations should be reconciled with the net operating income reported on the fund's operating statement (see Exhibit 2-12).

In addition to the combined statement of cash flows in the general-purpose financial statements, the comprehensive annual financial report should contain combining statements of cash flows for all individual proprietary and trust funds that operate on a business basis.

Nonprofit organizations such as hospitals generate income by selling goods and services. Operating results are reported in an income statement, and a statement of cash flows often is reported by these organizations. The content of these statements parallels that of proprietary and trust funds and of businesses. Other nonprofit organizations such as colleges and public service organizations do not report income in a business sense. Instead, they follow practices similar to those of governmental funds. Therefore, they normally do not report statements of cash flows.

[7]GASB, "Reporting Cash Flows of Proprietary and Nonexpendable Trust Funds and Governmental Entities That Use Proprietary Fund Accounting," *Statement No. 9,* September 1989.

EXHIBIT 2-12
CITY OF EAST RIVER
WATER AND SEWAGE FUND
STATEMENT OF CASH FLOWS FOR THE YEAR ENDED DECEMBER 31, 19X1
INCREASE (DECREASE) IN CASH AND CASH EQUIVALENTS

Cash flows from operating activities:		
Cash received from customers...	$ 850,000	
Cash paid to suppliers and employees	(715,000)	
Net cash provided by operating activities...............................		$ 135,000
Cash flows from noncapital financing activities:		
Net borrowings	$ 30,000	
Interest on borrowings	(2,500)	
Operating grants	65,000	
Net cash provided by noncapital financing activities		92,500
Cash flows from capital and related financing activities:		
Proceeds from sale of revenue bonds	$ 200,000	
Construction of capital assets...	(285,000)	
Principal paid on revenue bonds	(40,000)	
Interest paid on revenue bonds..	(3,000)	
Proceeds from sale of capital assets..	7,000	
Net cash used for capital and related financing activities		(121,000)
Cash flows from investing activities:		
Purchase of securities..	$(110,000)	
Proceeds from sale of investments...	30,000	
Interest and dividends on investments.......................................	8,000	
Net cash used in investing activities................................		(72,000)
Net increase in cash and cash equivalents..		$ 34,500
Cash and cash equivalents at beginning of year..		10,200
Cash and cash equivalents at end of year..		$ 44,700
Reconciliation of Net Operating Income to Net Cash Provided by Operating Activities:		
Net operating income		$ 56,000
Adjustments to reconcile net operating income to net cash provided by operating activities:		
Depreciation	$ 85,000	
Provision for uncollectible amounts	1,500	
Change in assets and liabilities:		
Increase in accounts receivable..	(12,000)	
Decrease in inventory	1,000	
Decrease in prepaid expenses...	600	
Increase in accounts payable	2,900	
Total adjustments..		79,000
Net cash provided by operating activities		$ 135,000

To summarize the financial statement requirements of nonprofit organizations, a list of required statements is provided in Exhibit 2-13.

DISCLOSURES AND SCHEDULES

As is true of business organizations, governments and other nonprofit organizations should provide notes to the financial statements to explain and expand the numerical information contained in the statements. These notes include a summary of **significant accounting policies** and disclosure of such matters as

1 Contingent liabilities
2 Encumbrances outstanding
3 Significant events subsequent to the balance sheet date that may have a bearing on financial operations
4 Pension plan obligations
5 Unpaid employee benefits such as vacation and sick leave
6 Violations of legal or contractual requirements of loans, grants, and similar activities
7 Debt service requirements until the maturity of outstanding debt
8 Commitments related to operating leases
9 Other commitments such as construction contracts

EXHIBIT 2-13
NONPROFIT ORGANIZATIONS
Schedule of Financial Statements

Colleges and universities:
  Balance sheet
  Statement of changes in fund balances
  Statement of current funds revenues, expenditures, and other changes
Hospitals:
  Balance sheet
  Statement of revenues and expenses
  Statement of changes in fund balances
  Statement of revenues and expenses and changes in unrestricted fund balance
  Statement of cash flow of unrestricted fund
Voluntary health and welfare organizations:
  Statement of support, revenue, and expenses and changes in fund balances
  Statement of functional expenses
  Balance sheet
Other not-for-profit organizations:
  Balance sheet
  Statement of activity, also referred to as statement of support, revenue, expenses, capital
    additions, and changes in fund balances
  May include statement of cash flow (not required)

Source: AICPA Industry Audit Guides.

10 Changes in general fixed assets and general long-term debt
11 Deficit balances in individual funds
12 Excesses of expenditures over amounts legally appropriated (approved) for expenditure in individual funds
13 Interfund receivables and payables

The specific content of the notes will vary among types of governmental and nonprofit organizations and will depend on specific circumstances. The overriding consideration is one of **full disclosure.** Sufficient information should be presented so that readers are well informed about the organization's resources, claims to resources, and changes in those resources.

Additional information also may be provided in annual financial reports, especially in the comprehensive annual financial report of a government. This additional information generally includes financial and demographic statistics for the last 10-year period. These schedules may include:

1 General governmental expenditures by function
2 General revenues by source
3 Property tax levies and collections
4 Assessed and estimated actual value of taxable property
5 Property tax rates for all overlapping governments (governments that include the same geographic area such as a county, a city, and a school district, all of which tax the same property)
6 Special assessment collections
7 The ratios of net general debt to assessed property values
8 Legal debt margins (how much debt can be issued before a legal maximum is reached)
9 Revenue bond coverage
10 Principal taxpayers
11 Other statistics

Not all of these schedules will be applicable to all governments.

OVERVIEW OF GOVERNMENTAL AND NONPROFIT FINANCIAL REPORTING

This chapter has described the primary financial reporting requirements for governmental and nonprofit organizations. The primary differences between governmental/nonprofit reports and those of business enterprises are attributable to the legal, political, and economic environment in which each operates. Important results of these differences are attributable to (1) the resulting emphasis on budgetary and fund control in the governmental and nonprofit environment and (2) a concern for matching the inflow and outflow of monetary resources available for use during the current fiscal period.

KEY CONCEPTS AND TERMS

Fund

Fund control

Expendable resources

Expenditure control

Budgetary control

Objectives of nonprofit financial reports

Comprehensive annual financial report

General-purpose financial statements

Governmental funds

Proprietary funds

Fiduciary funds

General fund

General revenues

Special revenue fund

Capital projects fund

Debt service fund

Enterprise fund

Internal service fund

Trust and agency funds

Expendable trust fund

Nonexpendable trust fund

Pension trust fund

Agency fund

General fixed asset account group

General long-term debt account group

Current unrestricted fund

Current restricted fund

Endowment fund

Plant fund

Loan fund

Basis of accounting for funds

Measurement focus

Accrual basis

Modified accrual basis

Flow of financial resources measurement focus

Financial resources

Intergenerational equity concept

Interperiod equity concept

Financial reporting pyramid

Combined statements

Combining statements

Fund balance

Reserve for supplies

Reserve for encumbrances

Fund equity

Specific-purpose funds

Plant replacement and expansion fund

Endowment funds

Annuity and life income fund

Expenditure

Expense

Other financing sources

Operating transfers

Encumbrances

Statement of revenues, expenditures, and changes in fund balance

Statement of revenues, expenditures, and changes in fund balance—budget compared with actual

Statement of cash flows

Significant accounting policies

Full disclosure

APPENDIX 2: Summary of GASB Financial Reporting Objectives[8] for State and Local Governmental Units

1 Financial reporting should provide a means of demonstrating accountability to the citizenry and enable the citizenry to assess that accountability by

a Demonstrating whether resources were obtained and used in accordance with the entity's legally adopted budget; it should also demonstrate compliance with other finance-related legal and contractual requirements.

[8]GASB *Codification*, Section 100.

b Providing information about the service efforts, costs, and accomplishments of the governmental entity.

2 Financial reporting should provide information necessary to evaluate the operating results of the governmental unit for the period by

 a Providing information about sources and uses of financial resources.

 b Providing information about how the governmental entity financed its activities and how it met its cash requirements.

 c Providing information necessary to determine whether the governmental entity's financial condition improved or deteriorated as a result of the year's operations.

3 Financial reporting should provide information necessary to assess the ability of a government to continue to finance its activities and meet its obligations by

 a Providing information about the financial condition, financial resources, and obligations of a governmental entity.

 b Disclosing legal or contractual restrictions placed on resources and the risk of potential loss of resources.

4 Financial reporting should provide information about the government's physical and other nonfinancial resources having useful lives that extend beyond the current accounting period, including information that can be used to assess the service potential of those resources.

DISCUSSION QUESTIONS

 1 How do the primary objectives of financial reporting differ between business and governmental or nonprofit organizations?

 2 Why are explicit controls more important in determining the format and procedures associated with governmental and nonprofit accounting than they are with business accounting?

 3 What are some of the explicit controls associated with governmental and nonprofit accounting? What is the purpose of each of these controls?

 4 Who are the primary users of governmental and nonprofit organization financial reports? What are the information needs of these users?

 5 Why is there less uniformity in the format and content of governmental and nonprofit financial reports than there is in business financial reports?

 6 What is a comprehensive annual financial report? How does it differ from general-purpose financial statements?

 7 What is an accounting fund? What is the purpose of fund accounting?

 8 What are the major types of funds used by state and local governments? Briefly describe the purpose of each type.

 9 What are general revenues? How do they differ from other revenues? What are the major sources of general revenues for governments?

 10 Which funds used by governments follow the capital maintenance concept? Which funds follow the intergenerational equity concept?

 11 How many funds should a local government use?

 12 What are the two account groups used by governments? How do these groups differ from funds?

 13 What fund types are used by hospitals, colleges, and other nonprofit organizations? What are the primary purposes of each of these fund types?

14 What do basis of accounting and measurement focus mean? What basis and focus are used for governmental funds?

15 What are the six levels of the financial reporting pyramid, and what is the purpose of each level?

16 What are combined financial statements? How do they differ from combining financial statements?

17 What major types of assets and liabilities would you expect to find in each of the funds and account groups of governmental units?

18 What is the purpose of a fund balance and what do reserves represent with respect to the fund balance?

19 What does the Total column of a combined balance sheet indicate? Why is the column marked "memorandum only"?

20 What basis of accounting characterizes accounting for hospitals? Why?

21 What kinds of assets and liabilities would you expect to find in the various funds of a hospital?

22 What are the primary sources of revenue for a governmental unit? What are the primary expenditure functions?

23 How do expenditures differ from expenses?

24 In what way are revenues and expenditures matched in governmental operating statements?

25 What are encumbrances? Why are they important in accounting for governmental units?

26 How are the operating statements of hospitals and colleges and universities similar to and different from those of governmental units? Why do these similarities and differences exist?

27 What is the purpose of comparing budgeted with actual revenues and expenditures?

28 When should a statement of cash flows be used by governmental and nonprofit organizations? What is the purpose of this statement?

EXERCISES

1 Identify the funds and/or account groups that would be used by a governmental unit to account for each of the following events:
a Approval of the general revenue budget
b Collection of property taxes
c Issuance of long-term debt to be repaid from general revenues
d Receipt of revenues that can be used only for street maintenance
e Expenditures made for the construction of a new municipal building
f Completion of a new municipal building
g Money set aside for repayment of principal and interest on general debt
h Revenue received by the data processing department from sale of services to other departments of the government
i Expenses recorded by a municipally owned garage that provides parking for local citizens
j Taxes collected by a county for cities in the county
k Amounts received from employees for their retirement
l Donation of money by a local citizen to be invested, with the earnings used to purchase equipment for the city recreation department
m Long-term debt issued by a public utility

2 Identify the local government funds or account groups in which you would expect to find each of the following accounts:

    a Amount available for repayment of long-term debt
    b Construction in progress
    c General obligation bonds payable
    d Accumulated depreciation
    e Buildings
    f Revenue bonds payable
    g Investment in general fixed assets
    h Retained earnings

3 In which governmental unit funds or account groups would you expect to find the following accounts?
    a Property tax revenue
    b Expenditure for debt retirement
    c Charges to customers
    d Public safety expenditures
    e Interest expense
    f Net income
    g Expenditure for equipment
    h Depreciation expense

4 Identify the funds that would be used by a university to account for each of the following events:
    a Tuition received from students.
    b A donation was received to establish an endowed professorship.
    c Loans are paid to students.
    d Salaries are paid to faculty.
    e Expenditures are incurred for the construction of a new building.
    f The cost of room and board is charged to students living in university dormitories.
    g Unrestricted gifts are received from alumni.
    h Money is received from faculty that will be transferred to the state retirement fund.

5 Identify the funds that would be used by a hospital to account for the following events:
    a Patients are billed for services.
    b Endowment income is earned.
    c Donations are received to purchase equipment.
    d A grant is received for the operation of a cancer treatment center.
    e Fixed assets are purchased.
    f Depreciation is recorded.
    g The hospital board of directors designates money to be used for equipment purchases.
    h Operating expenses are paid.

6 Indicate the fund(s) or account group(s) which most likely would be used to record each of the following transactions for (1) a local government, (2) a public university, and (3) a public hospital.
    a Receipt of general revenues
    b Receipt of resources restricted to externally designated purposes
    c Receipt of resources for management-designated purposes
    d Receipt of resources restricted to construction of new buildings
    e Receipt of resources restricted to endowment
    f Receipt of resources that must be transferred to external parties
    g Receipt of resources that will be used to pay for debt principal and interest
    h Acquisition of fixed assets for use in general operations
    i Issuance of long-term debt to be repaid by general revenues

PROBLEMS

1 A list of accounts and account balances at June 30, 19X1, is presented below for the City of South Hill. All accounts have normal balances. The City has a general fund, a debt service fund, a capital projects fund, an enterprise fund to account for the water department, and general fixed asset and general long-term debt account groups.

Account title	Balance
Accounts Receivable (water department)	$ 1,100
Amount Available for Payment of Debt	17,500
Amount to Be Provided for Payment of Debt	132,500
Buildings (water department)	35,000
Accumulated Depreciation—Buildings	12,000
Buildings (general government)	140,000
Cash (general government)	8,000
Cash (for payment of debt service)	6,000
Cash (for capital projects)	4,000
Cash (water department)	3,200
Construction-in-Progress (general government)	6,000
Donated Capital (water department)	10,000
Due from Other Governments (general government)	2,200
Due from Other Governments (capital projects)	5,000
General Obligation Bonds Payable	150,000
Improvements Other than Buildings (general)	85,000
Interest payable (water department)	3,200
Investments (general government)	10,000
Investments (for debt service)	14,000
Investment in General Fixed Assets	316,000
Land (general government)	20,000
Land (water department)	8,000
Machinery and Equipment (general)	65,000
Machinery and Equipment (water department)	26,000
Accumulated Depreciation—Machinery and Equipment	4,600
Matured Bonds Payable	16,000
Matured Interest Payable	2,500
Reserve for Encumbrances (general government)	850
Reserve for Encumbrances (capital projects)	1,800
Reserve for Supplies	700
Retained Earnings	2,910
Revenue Bonds Payable	40,000
Supplies Inventory (general government)	700
Supplies Inventory (water department)	200
Taxes Receivable (general government)	2,000
Vouchers Payable (general government)	5,500
Vouchers Payable (water department)	790
Undesignated Fund Balances (all funds)	?

Required:

a Prepare a combined balance sheet for the City of South Hill for 19X1.
b Discuss the types of assets and liabilities reported by each fund type. Why are these assets and liabilities reported in this manner instead of in one fund?

c Explain the purpose of each of the following accounts and why each is reported in a specific type of fund or account group:

Construction-in-Progress
Amount Available for Payment of Debt
Amount to Be Provided for Payment of Debt
Matured Bonds Payable
Matured Interest Payable
Investment in General Fixed Assets
Reserve for Encumbrances
Reserve for Supplies

2 A list of accounts and account balances at September 30, 19X1, is presented below for the City of West Lake. All accounts have normal balances. The city accounts for parking revenues in a special revenue fund which is used to pay for all of the city's highway and street improvements. The city also maintains a general fund, a debt service fund, and a capital projects fund. A general fixed asset account group and a general long-term debt account group are used for their appropriate purposes.

Account title	Balance
Capital Outlay (for capital projects)	$54,500
Charges for Services (general government)	4,000
Charges for Services (parking fees)	6,000
Debt Service—Payment of Principal	9,250
Debt service—Payment of Interest	2,750
Education Expenditures	16,000
Fines Revenue	2,000
Fund Balance—Oct. 1, 19X0 (general fund)	8,400
Fund Balance—Oct. 1, 19X0 (special revenues)	3,400
Fund Balance—Oct. 1, 19X0 (debt service)	685
Fund Balance—Oct. 1, 19X0 (capital projects)	1,300
Fund Balance—Sept. 30, 19X1 (all funds)	?
General Government Expenditures	14,000
Health Expenditures	7,500
Highways and Streets Expenditures	26,500
Intergovernmental Revenue (general government)	8,000
Intergovernmental Revenue (for streets)	4,000
Intergovernmental revenue (for capital projects)	20,000
Licenses Revenues	14,000
Operating Transfers In (for streets)	4,500
Operating Transfers In (for debt service)	6,000
Operating Transfers In (for capital projects)	5,000
Operating Transfer Out (from general government)	15,500
Proceeds of General Obligation Bonds (for capital projects)	30,000
Public Safety Expenditures	18,000
Recreation Expenditures	8,000
Sanitation Expenditures	9,500
Taxes Revenues (general government)	70,000
Taxes Revenues (for streets)	12,000
Taxes Revenues (for debt service)	8,000
Welfare Expenditures	10,000

Required:

a Prepare a combined statement of revenues, expenditures, and changes in fund balances for all governmental fund types for the year ended September 30, 19X1.

b How would you interpret the results of West Lake's governmental funds with respect to the capital maintenance and intergenerational equity concepts?

3 The accounts and account balances which follow are for the enterprise and internal service funds of the City of West Lake at September 30, 19X1. All accounts have normal balances.

Account title	Balance
Depreciation Expense (enterprise)	$ 3,650
Depreciation Expense (internal service)	450
Operating Grants (enterprise)	6,000
Personal Service Expenses (enterprise)	22,500
Personal Service Expenses (internal service)	8,700
Retained Earnings, Oct. 1, 19X0 (enterprise)	2,300
Retained Earnings, Oct. 1, 19X0 (internal service)	785
Service Revenue (enterprise)	32,000
Service Revenue (internal service)	12,000
Supplies Expense (enterprise)	6,750
Supplies Expense (internal service)	1,300
Utilities Expense (enterprise)	5,300
Utilities Expense (internal service)	875

Required:

a Prepare a combined statement of revenues, expenditures, and changes in fund balances for all governmental fund types for the year ended September 30, 19X1.

b How would you interpret the results of operations for the West Lake proprietary funds with respect to the capital maintenance concept?

4 The following information is provided for the Southwest County general fund on December 31, 19X1. All accounts have normal balances.

Account title	Actual	Budget
Charges for Services	$ 46,000	$ 44,000
Education Expenditures	678,000	675,000
Fines	23,000	25,000
Fund Balance, Jan. 1, 19X1	178,000	178,000
General Government Expenditures	137,000	140,000
Health Expenditures	79,000	76,000
Highways Expenditures	103,000	100,000
Intergovernmental Revenues	155,000	155,000
License Revenues	149,000	140,000
Parks and Recreation	62,000	60,000
Public Safety Expenditures	210,000	200,000
Taxes	992,000	998,000
Transfers Out	91,000	100,000

Required:

a Prepare a statement of revenues, expenditures, and changes in fund balance—budget and actual for the general fund.

b How and to whom is the information reported in this statement useful?

5 Information is presented below for Central County Hospital. All accounts have normal balances on June 30, 19X1. All accounts relate to current unrestricted operations except as noted.

Account title	Balance
Accounts Payable	$ 72,000
Accounts Receivable—Net	46,000
Bonds Payable—Noncurrent	220,000
Bonds Payable—Current	40,000
Cash (unrestricted)	22,000
Cash (board-designated)	7,000
Cash (plant replacement and expansion)	8,000
Cash (endowment)	18,000
Inventories	23,000
Investments (board-designated)	90,000
Investments (plant replacement and expansion)	168,000
Investments (endowment)	450,000
Land, Buildings, and Equipment	856,000
Accumulated Depreciation	342,000
Notes Payable—Current	50,000
Prepaid Expenses	13,000
Fund Balance—June 30, 19X1 (all funds)	?

Required:

a Prepare a balance sheet for Central County Hospital at June 30, 19X1.

b Describe the principal differences between the balance sheet for Central County Hospital and a balance sheet for a typical business organization. Why do these differences exist?

6 Listed below are accounts and account balances for Southwest County Hospital for the year ended March 31, 19X1. All account balances are normal.

Account title	Balance
Administrative Services Expense	$ 250,000
Allowance for Uncollectibles	75,000
General Services Expense	140,000
Interest Expense	56,000
Nursing Services Expense	437,000
Other Operating Revenues	124,000
Other Professional Services	230,000
Patient Service Revenues	810,000
Provision for Depreciation	212,000
Unrestricted Donations	144,000
Unrestricted Endowment Income	109,000

Required:

a Prepare a statement of revenues and expenses for Southwest County Hospital for the year ended March 31, 19X1.

b How would you interpret the results of operations for the hospital with respect to the capital maintenance concept?

3

Using Governmental and Nonprofit Financial Reports

A major goal of the first three chapters of this text is to explain the rationale underlying governmental and nonprofit accounting and financial reporting. This chapter examines the uses that are made of governmental and nonprofit financial information. The information needs of various users will be considered along with how financial report data can be used to meet these needs. An examination of the use of financial report data will contribute to an understanding of governmental and nonprofit financial reporting.

This chapter is divided into four sections that discuss the information needs of the primary users of governmental and nonprofit financial reports—creditors, granting agencies, oversight groups, and constituents. The information needs of these groups will be outlined, and ways that financial report data may be used to meet the needs of these users will be described.

CREDITOR INFORMATION NEEDS

Creditors are major resource providers to many governmental and nonprofit organizations. **Creditors** include bondholders and financial institutions that lend money to these organizations. Since organizations depend on creditors for resources, they are concerned about providing data that creditors can use to make lending decisions. If these data were not provided, creditors would seek alternative sources of information or would seek alternative investments for which information was available. If information needed by creditors is not readily available, investments in these organizations become more risky for investors who are less certain about the prospects for timely repayment of principal and interest. Accordingly, we should anticipate that creditors will demand a higher rate of return on investments in organizations with incomplete financial information than they would if needed information were available.

Creditors lend money to an organization in order to earn a return on their investments. In order to assess whether or not to make the loan, creditors must assess the risks associated with the loan. One type of risk is **default risk** which is the probability that the principal and interest on the loan will not be repaid in a timely manner. Creditors will demand a higher rate of return (effective interest rate) on debt that is assessed to have a higher default risk relative to lower-risk debt. Default results when an organization does not have sufficient cash available to meet its current obligations, including payment of interest and principal for its debt. Accordingly, a major information need for creditors is to determine the cash flow prospects of an organization over the period in which the debt will be repaid.

A variety of creditor relationships are possible for governmental and nonprofit organizations. Loans may be for short periods of time to meet resource needs in anticipation of forthcoming revenues. For example, a city may issue tax anticipation notes to a local bank that will be repaid when property taxes are received. On the other hand, loans may be for long periods of time—10, 20, or 30 years. These long-term loans are frequently used to construct or purchase long-lived assets.

Often the length of the loan is established to coincide approximately with the life of the asset that is being financed. The concept of intergenerational equity supports the issuance of debt that corresponds in maturity with the life of the assets acquired with the debt proceeds. If the principal and interest on the debt are repaid over the useful life of the asset, the recipients of the benefits of use of the assets will pay for the cost of the assets by repaying the debt. Furthermore, the intergenerational equity concept limits the purpose for which long-term debt should be issued. Under this concept, the debt should be used only for acquiring long-term assets. Moreover, it should not be used to pay for current operations that provide benefits only in the short run. The use of long-term debt to pay for current services shifts the cost of the services to future generations.

Long-term loans may be repaid from **general revenues** of the organization such as property taxes, membership fees, or patient charges. Alternatively, the loans may be repaid from profits earned by specific segments of the organization. For example, government enterprise funds may issue debt for construction projects that will be repaid from profits earned by the operation of the project once it is completed. Bonds which are to be repaid by government general fund revenues are known as **general obligation bonds.** Bonds that are to be repaid from the operations of government enterprises are known as **revenue bonds.**

One of the purposes of fund accounting is to provide creditors with information about short-term versus long-term cash flow prospects and to distinguish enterprise operations from general government operations. Since the general fund of a government accounts only for short-term resources and obligations, an examination of the fund assets, liabilities, revenues, and expenditures provides information concerning the liquidity of the entity. If assets and prospective revenues are not sufficient to retire liabilities and pay for prospective expenditures during the current fiscal year, the government may have difficulty in meeting all of its cash flow requirements. Many of the expenditure items of an organization are relatively fixed—salaries, lease payments, purchase commitments, etc.—reducing the flexibility of the organization if resource inflows are not as large as anticipated. By segregating restricted resources from unrestricted resources and by segregating current from noncurrent assets and liabilities, governmental and nonprofit organizations provide creditors a means for evaluating expected cash flows that may be available for specific purposes, including payment of principal and interest.

Revenue Debt

The fund structure of governmental and nonprofit organizations permits purchasers of revenue bonds to focus on the profitability of the organizations or enterprises that will service the bonds. In particular, government enterprise funds report the financial position, results of operations, and changes in cash flows of these entities independently of other government operations. Since the entities are similar in many ways to businesses, investing in the debt of these entities requires similar analysis expertise to investing in corporate debt. (The reader should recall that enterprise funds operate with a capital maintenance goal in a separable product or service environment.)

Financial ratios similar to those used by corporate investors (for example, times interest earned, return on assets, and debt to equity) can be used by investors in revenue bonds. **Financial ratios** provide a means of comparing resources and resource flows of organizations by expressing the resources and flows on a basis relative to the size of the organization or to the magnitude of other resources or flows.

Bonded debt issued by governmental and nonprofit organizations (like that issued by corporations) is often rated by a service such as Standard and Poor's Corporation or Moody's Investor Services. **Bond ratings** issued by these organizations provide an assessment of the default risk associated with the bonds. These rating agencies identify certain financial data as being important for their assessments. Some of the information used in these assessments is described below.

Debt Service Capacity   **Debt service** is defined as the amount of annual principal and interest payments. **Debt service capacity** is the ability of an organization to meet its debt service requirements. It can be measured by the annual earnings of an organization divided by the debt service requirement. For example, if bonds are issued by a municipally owned utility to build an electric generating plant, the earnings from selling electric power to customers is used to pay the interest and principal on the debt. If $1,000,000 of bonds are issued, the bonds pay interest at 8 percent, $50,000 of bonds are repaid each year, and the utility earns $250,000 in the first year of operation, the debt service ratio for the first year would be $250,000/($80,000 + $50,000) = 1.92.

As this ratio becomes smaller, the risk that the utility will be unable to retire principal and interest on a timely basis becomes greater. Creditors want to know if the project will earn a sufficient amount to service the debt issued to build the project. Accordingly, information about projected earnings and debt service costs is important in determining whether the project should be initiated and bonds should be issued. Also, if the entity decides to issue new debt for plant replacement or expansion, information about past debt service coverage will be needed in order to determine the feasibility of new projects.

The ratio of long-term debt to fixed assets and the ratio of changes in long-term debt to changes in fixed assets provide information about the entity's debt management. If these ratios are large relative to those of other similar entities or become larger over time, the entity may be having difficulty in meeting its current operating needs. Long-term debt normally is issued for the purchase or construction of long-term assets. If debt is increasing relative to the level of assets, some of the inflow of cash is being used for current operations rather than to acquire fixed assets in violation of intergenerational equity concept.

Revenue Stability   In examining the ability of an organization to support debt service for revenue bonds, consideration should be given to the **stability of revenue sources** of the entity. Are the organization's revenues susceptible to major fluctuations with changing economic conditions? Defaults on bonds normally occur during major downturns in the economy. Therefore, creditors will be interested in the sensitivity of earnings to downward swings in the economy. This sensitivity can be assessed by examining past associations between revenues or earnings and economic indicators such as per capita income, unemployment levels, or regional productivity indicators. Also, the nature of the revenue source provides information about sensitivity. When income declines, consumers are likely to forego certain activities, such as some types of recreation. They may be less able to forego the use of electricity or water. Other types of activities may actually gain in use in periods of economic downturn. For example, more people may use public transportation when their income levels decline. In general, levels of earnings and operating income that are not sensitive to changes in general economic conditions are positive signals. The use of nonoperating income or unplanned transfers from other funds to avoid a deficit suggests financial problems.

Rates for Public Services   The profitability of public enterprises depends on the efficiency of providing the services as well as the rates charged to customers. Rates for many government enterprises are set by a municipal council or by a commission appointed to oversee rate structures. If the earnings of an entity decline so that repayment of principal becomes a problem, the entity may be able to increase the price customers are required to pay. However, if rates are already high relative to similar entities in other locations, it may be difficult to obtain approval for price increases. Therefore, information about the rates charged to customers relative to charges for similar enterprises in the region is important in determining the ability of the entity to raise additional revenues in the future if the need arises.

Reserve Funds Governmental enterprises often establish investment accounts or **sinking funds** to accumulate resources that can be used for debt service coverage if a financial emergency arises. The ratio of the amount available in these investment accounts to the annual amount of principal and interest payments on the entity's debt is a measure of the protection available to creditors from these reserves.

Liquidity Positive cash flows and favorable liquidity ratios indicate the entity's ability to meet current obligations. **Liquidity** is a measure of the ability of an organization to generate cash to meet current operating needs. Use of debt to provide cash for current operations or declining trends in the current ratio (current assets/current liabilities) signals potential financial difficulty. Accounts receivable turnover (operating revenue/net receivables) is another measure of liquidity. Persistently large balances in receivables suggest difficulty in cash collection. In an economic downturn, many receivables may prove to be uncollectible, resulting in cash flow problems for the organization.

Other Indicators Financial information is only part of the set of information used by creditors and rating agencies in evaluating governmental and nonprofit debt. Numerous other data may be examined relating to the economic attributes of the organization and the geographic region in which it is located, for example, management quality, bond covenants, and the use of independent audits. Thus, financial information may be compared with other attributes in order to assess the financial strength of an organization.

General Obligation Debt

The evaluation of general obligation debt for governmental units is somewhat different from the analysis of revenue debt since general resource flows rather than operating profits are used to service the debt. An overall appraisal of the fiscal viability of an organization is necessary. This appraisal depends heavily on trends in the organization's **demographic and socioeconomic attributes** (such as the size, composition, and income levels of the population) that would suggest likely changes in resource base or service demands. Some of the measures suggested for evaluating general obligation debt are discussed below.

The Magnitude of General Obligation Debt The ratio of total general obligation debt to total general revenues or population is a measure of the size of the debt relative to the size of the local government. This ratio can be compared to that of other governments or trends in the ratio can be examined over time. Large or increasing ratios indicate declining financial condition. The size of the debt balance relative to the resource base of the government is the relevant measure in assessing debt magnitude. Governments that have larger tax bases are more capable of supporting large amounts of debt than are other governments. The amount of annual general fund revenues on total market value of property is a reasonable measure of the size of the tax base.

Other important measures of the magnitude of the debt that can be supported by a government are the amount or percentage of principal and interest that must be repaid each year for the next five to ten years relative to the total debt and interest to be paid over the interval and the amount of sinking or reserve funds that are available relative to the amount of debt. Since general obligation debt is repaid from general revenues, a fairly constant ratio of debt service to general fund revenues should be observed over time. If unusually large amounts of debt are to be repaid in a specific year, a sinking or reserve fund account should be accumulating the money that will be needed for these payments.

Another important measure is the magnitude of overlapping debt to be repaid by the government's taxpayers. **Overlapping debt** arises when taxpayers are responsible for debt issued by several governmental units such as a city, a county, and a school district. The property taxes paid by the residents of a particular location may be the source of funding for debt issued by all of these governmental entities. It is important to assess the total tax burden that is imposed on the tax base in determining how much debt can be supported.

Legal Debt Limits   A **legal debt limit** often is imposed on governments, either by higher levels of government or by the government's own statutory requirements. The ratio of the current amount of debt outstanding to the legal debt limit measures the ability of the government to issue additional debt. The ratio also measures the magnitude of the debt relative to the level of debt that local authorities consider to be reasonable. As a government nears its legal limit, constraints may be imposed on the government's ability to meet service demands. These constraints may lead to declining service levels, population movement, and financial difficulties. It is important for a government to manage its debt wisely to make sure that the debt is used only for appropriate reasons.

General Revenue Structure   The ability of a government to continue to raise sufficient revenues to meet the service needs of its citizens and to repay its obligations is an important attribute in assessing credit risk. The levels of tax rates relative to other governments and changes in these rates over time indicate the ability of the government to generate higher levels of taxes in the future if the need arises. If tax rates already are high, taxpayers are likely to be unwilling to pay higher taxes in the future. The percentage rates for income taxes and sales taxes are measures of the current tax burden. The amount of property tax charged per $1,000 of assessed property value is another measure of tax burden.

The ratio of the assessed value of property to the market value of the property is another measure of **taxing capacity** of the government. Property taxes can be increased either by increasing the tax rate or by increasing the ratio of assessed value to market value. If this ratio is already high, the government has less flexibility to increase the ratio in the future as a means of raising additional taxes.

The percentage of tax levies collected is another measure of the government's effectiveness. Large amounts of uncollected taxes indicate that the government is not properly supervising collections or that taxpayers are unable or unwilling to pay their taxes. The failure to pay taxes can signal difficulties in the local economy or taxpayer concerns about the fairness of the tax structure. In either case, the ability of the government to provide revenues to meet its obligations may be questionable.

The sources and variability of general fund revenues is another measure of the government's ability to provide for its cash flow requirements. Some taxes increase in relation to changing economic conditions. For example, increases in inflation will result in increases in personal income. Accordingly, income tax revenues will increase as well. On the other hand, property taxes remain relatively constant until the property is either sold or reassessed. The mix of revenue sources used by a government is a measure of the sensitivity of the government's revenues to changing economic conditions. Also, the use of large amounts of intergovernmental revenues can be risky. The programs that provide these revenues generally are outside of the control of the receiving government. If the programs are cut or are eliminated, the government may have difficulty covering the costs of these programs. While some of the services provided by the programs may be eliminated, the government may have difficulty eliminating all of the services because of citizen demand. In addition, revenues that are restricted for special purposes or that are nonrecurring should be separated from other general revenues in assessing the ability of a government to meet its current service demands and debt service requirements.

Expenditure Requirements Certain types of government expenditures are easier to control than others. Expenditures for certain services such as current operations for police and fire protection, sanitation, education, and health care are difficult to reduce since the underlying services are necessary. Other expenditures for services such as recreational activities or for capital improvements such as new buildings and equipment are more easily foregone in a financial distress situation. Therefore, the ratio of **discretionary** to **nondiscretionary expenditures** measures the flexibility of a government to an economic downturn. However, if a government is consistently foregoing capital expenditures and expenditures for maintenance and upkeep of its fixed assets, it is probably already facing financial problems.

The inability of a government to meet all of its current cash flow needs can be measured by the ratio of general fund revenues to general fund expenditures, by recurring deficits in the general fund, and by the existence of short-term debt outstanding at fiscal year-end. The ratio of current general fund revenues to expenditures should be close to 1. However, if this ratio is much below 1 or is persistently below 1 over several years, the government is likely to be facing financial problems. This condition also can be observed if the fund balance for the general fund is negative. While governments often borrow on a short-term basis to meet current cash flow needs pending tax collections, these obligations should be repaid from current period revenues. If the government is unable to repay its short-term debt from current revenues, it is likely to be facing considerable cash flow problems.

Other Liabilities Governments often incur liabilities other than bonded debt. Some of these liabilities require careful scrutiny in order to determine their potential effect on the government's future cash flows. For example, governments generally provide retirement and other postemployment benefits for their employees. Employees earn these benefits while they are employed by the government. The compensation is not paid to the employees until they retire. However, the government is incurring a liability for these future payments. This liability may be offset by investments the government makes each year as employees earn these benefits. If the government fails to make sufficient investments to cover these future costs, revenues in future periods will have to be used to pay these benefits. Therefore, the ratio of **unfunded pension and other postemployment plan liabilities** to general fund revenues is an indication of the magnitude of these demands on cash flows.

Other liabilities can result from contractual commitments and contingencies that the government has outstanding. Information about purchase contracts, pending litigation, and insurance coverage is useful for assessing whether future cash flows may be required to pay for existing commitments or contingencies.

Warning Signals Standard and Poor's specifies 15 warning signals that it believes are especially critical in assessing general obligation debt.[1] These are shown in Exhibit 3-1. A scan of these items, in addition to the previous discussion, indicates the importance of accounting information in credit analysis. Fixed benchmarks do not exist for many of the ratios or numbers that are shown in these lists. Individual judgment is necessary in comparing numbers for various organizations. The ratios and numbers are useful primarily on a relative basis when compared to other similar organizations or when compared over time for a given organization.

---

[1]For further discussion see H. Sherwood, *How Corporate and Municipal Debt Is Rated*, Wiley, New York, 1976.

EXHIBIT 3-1
STANDARD AND POOR'S FINANCIAL WARNING INDICATORS FOR GOVERNMENTAL UNITS

1. Current year operating deficit
2. Consecutive years of operating fund deficit
3. Current general fund deficit (two or more years in last five)
4. Short-term debt (other than bond anticipation notes) at end of fiscal year greater than 5% of main operating fund revenues
5. Short-term interest and current year debt service greater than 20% of total revenues
6. Total property tax collections less than 92% of total levy
7. Declining market valuations–two consecutive years or a three-year trend
8. Overall net debt ratio 50% higher than four years ago
9. Current year operating deficit larger than previous year's deficit
10. General fund deficit in the current year
11. Two-year trend of increasing short-term debt outstanding at fiscal year-end
12. Property taxes greater than 90% of tax limit
13. Net debt outstanding greater than 90% of tax limit
14. A trend of decreasing tax collections—two consecutive years or a three-year trend
15. Overall net debt ratio 20% higher than previous year

Rating agencies and individual investors are concerned with evaluating alternatives. Creditors select investment opportunities from among alternative organizations. Comparison is an important part of this process. In order to make meaningful comparisons, creditors are interested in determining the risk associated with alternative investments. Bond ratings provide one means of assessing relative default risk.

Market Risk   Default risk is not the only risk of concern to creditors. A creditor may not earn an expected rate of return on an investment even if the issuer pays all of its principal and interest on a timely basis. If the creditor decides to sell the investment prior to its maturity in order to use the cash proceeds for some other purpose, the amount received will depend on market conditions for the investment at the time of the sale. Thus, some creditors are concerned about being able to sell their investments before they mature and the susceptibility of the investments to changing market conditions. Many banks, insurance companies, and other institutional investors who frequently buy and sell debt securities maintain departments specifically for the purpose of evaluating the market risk of alternative investments.

Market risk can be measured by the variability of bond prices over time. The more variability in the prices relative to changes in general economic conditions (as observed, for example, in interest rates), the more risk is inherent in an investment. The primary determinant of market risk is the maturity of the debt. Shifts in current economic conditions have a more pronounced effect on debt with longer maturity relative to that with shorter maturity.

Market risk is not independent of default risk and, therefore, the same kind of information can be used in assessing market risk as is used for assessing default risk. For example, certain financial ratios have been shown to be associated with market risk. These ratios include long-term debt, short-term debt, intergovernmental revenue, capital expenditures, and property taxes expressed as a percentage of total revenues. The total revenue variable in these ratios is used to adjust for differences in the size of the resource base of different municipalities. The importance of these ratios results from the risk associated with different types of revenue sources and expenditure categories. This risk results because some revenues and expenditures may change at a faster rate than others and some are more controllable by government officials than others.

Example Financial Ratios

Any number of financial ratios can be calculated from governmental and nonprofit financial reports. Exhibit 3-2 describes a number of ratios that have been suggested for analyzing nonprofit financial data.[2] These ratios are primarily for

---

EXHIBIT 3-2

SAMPLE FINANCIAL RATIOS FOR NONPROFIT ORGANIZATIONS

---

1. Current ratio (current assets/current liabilities)
2. Quick ratio (cash, marketable securities, and accounts receivable/current liabilities)
3. Acid-test ratio (cash and marketable securities/current liabilities)
4. Days in client or patient accounts receivables (net client or patient account receivables/net service revenue × 360 days)
5. Average payment period ratio (current liabilities/operating expenses less depreciation)
6. Days cash on hand ratio (cash and marketable securities/operating expenses less depreciation × 360 days)
7. Equity financing ratio (fund balance/total assets)
8. Cash flow to total debt ratio (excess of revenues over expenses and depreciation/current liabilities and long-term debt)
9. Long-term debt to equity ratio (long-term liabilities/fund balance)
10. Fixed asset financing ratio (long-term liabilities/net fixed assets)
11. Times interest earned ratio (excess of revenues over [expenses less interest expense]/interest expense)
12. Debt service coverage ratio (cash flow and interest expense/principal payment and interest expense)
13. Total asset turnover ratio (total operating revenue/total assets)
14. Fixed asset turnover ratio (total operating revenue/net fixed assets)
15. Current asset turnover ratio (total operating revenue/current assets)
16. Operating margin ratio (total operating revenue less operating expenses/total operating revenue)
17. Return on total asset ratio (excess of revenue over expenses/total assets)
18. Return on equity ratio (excess of revenues over expenses/fund balance)
19. Average age of plant ratio (accumulated depreciation/depreciation expense)
20. Restricted equity ratio (total restricted fund balances/unrestricted fund balance)

---

[2]For additional discussion see W. Cleverley, *Financial Analysis Service: User's Guide,* Healthcare Financial Management Association, 1983.

organizations that earn revenues from the sale of goods and services and are interested in capital maintenance.

Financial statement analysis is not an exact science. A considerable amount of individual judgment is required. What one analyst considers to be important, another may consider unimportant. However, patterns of financial ratios that describe the performance of one organization relative to others or relative to industry-wide trends and trends in ratios over time play a role in the investment decision process. Investors and rating agencies appear to take note of ratios or trends that depart excessively from the norm. Particular interest focuses on the amount of debt an organization has outstanding relative to its resource base and on changes in the resource base, since these factors ultimately determine the probability that principal and interest will be paid when due.

INFORMATION FOR THIRD-PARTY PAYMENT DECISIONS

Grants and other third-party payments constitute a large portion of the resource inflows of many governmental and nonprofit organizations. Local governments receive grants from state and federal programs. Private foundations provide grants to many nonprofit organizations. Sometimes grants may be used at the discretion of the organization with few restrictions from the grantor. However, in many cases the grant is for a specific project or purpose. The conditions of the grant must be met or the grant funds must be returned to the grantor. Thus, two primary dimensions of grant accounting exist: (1) an organization must be able to account for the receipt and use of grant resources to demonstrate compliance with grant requirements, and (2) an organization must be able to demonstrate a need for a grant and the ability to manage grant resources.

Demonstrating Compliance

The first of these dimensions is apparent in the structure of governmental and nonprofit accounting. Separate funds frequently are used to account for grants. Governments use special revenue and trust funds for this purpose. Other nonprofit organizations use restricted funds such as special-purpose or plant funds. The fund used depends on the purpose of the grant. Accounting systems must be capable of identifying costs associated with grant-funded projects. Often grants provide for reimbursement of approved costs. Therefore, an organization must maintain a record of these reimbursable costs. If a grant requires that resources be used for specified services or for services to certain individuals, the accounting system must demonstrate that these requirements have been met. Fund accounting is one means of segregating resources in order to demonstrate that the resources were used for the intended purpose during the appropriate time period.

Grants have had a major impact on auditing in the governmental and nonprofit sector. Demonstrating compliance with grant requirements is as much an auditing as an accounting matter. Independent audits provide confirmation of proper grant accounting and use of grant resource. The federal government requires, as a part of its "single audit" legislation, independent audits of all state and local governments that receive more than $25,000 in federal grants.[3] In turn, audits have an effect on accounting since auditors may identify weaknesses in accounting systems or noncompliance with GAAP requirements. A brief description of the auditing environment for governmental and nonprofit organizations is provided in the Appendix to this chapter.

Federal and state transfers are also a major source of resource inflows for nonprofit organizations such as hospitals and universities. Medicare and medicaid programs as well as other **third-party provider** (someone other than the service recipient) payments, such as those from insurance companies, account for a large portion of hospital revenues. Similar accounting and auditing requirements are imposed on recipients as for grant programs. Nonprofit reports are frequently designed for the needs of external providers to show that grant resources have been properly used and to determine reimbursements for incurred costs. These reports may include information in addition to the basic financial statements described in earlier chapters.

Demonstrating Need and Capacity

The other dimension of grant accounting is similar to that of accounting to creditors. Governmental and nonprofit organizations are evaluated by granting agencies to determine the need for grant money and the ability to use the money consistent with the purposes of the grant. The purposes of grants may differ considerably. Some grants are intended to produce results which benefit the granting organization. These grantors search for recipients who are most likely to produce the desired result. Other grants are designed to assist organizations which lack a sufficient resource base to provide certain services on their own or to equalize the availability of services across organizations or locations. Also, grants often are provided on a matching basis, with the grantor providing some percentage of the total project costs if the recipient can demonstrate a capacity to provide the remaining portion. Accordingly, governmental and nonprofit accounting systems may be called on to provide financial information to show fiscal needs as well as fiscal capacity.

The basic financial reports of governmental and nonprofit organizations provide some of the information used by granting agencies in making grant decisions. Comparison of resources across organizations, changes in resources over time, the use of resources in meeting current service demands, and the ability of management to meet budget projections and to use available resources efficiently provide information for allocating some grant resources.

---

[3]The term "single audit" refers to the requirement for a simultaneous or "single" audit of all departments or programs of a state or local government receiving federal funds in place of a prior requirement that each department receiving federal funds be audited individually.

Ratios which disclose the composition of revenues, expenditures by function, debt burden, and differences between actual and budgeted amounts are consistent with these information needs. These ratios can be compared across organizations just as they are for creditor decisions. As was true for creditors, financial information is only part of the total information used in making grant decisions.

OVERSIGHT GROUP INFORMATION NEEDS

Organizations hire managers to oversee their daily operations and to make the decisions necessary for the organization to continue to operate. However, managers do not have total discretion over the decision-making process, especially for major decisions that affect the long-run strategies of the organization. Managers are responsible for reporting to oversight groups who represent the owners, contributors, or taxpayers of the organization.

In businesses, the primary oversight group is the board of directors whose members are elected by the stockholders as their representatives to approve management decisions and to oversee management activities. Management must get board approval for certain decisions, and the board can make changes in management personnel and set policy on behalf of stockholders.

Constituents of nonprofit organizations also elect boards of directors. The supporters of these organizations elect representatives to make decisions about hiring managers and to approve of management decisions. Managers are required to report to the board about the financial condition and activities of the organization. The board approves budgets and authorizes major expenditures and programs.

The representation process is very formalized for governmental organizations. Each level of government is separated into executive and legislative branches. The executive branch is responsible for making management decisions to carry out the ongoing activities of the government. These political managers may be elected as in the case of the President of the United States, the governors of the states, and the mayors of many cities. In some cases, they are hired by the legislators as in the case of city or county managers.

Regardless of how the chief executive officer is selected, each level of government has an elected representative body. The U.S. Congress, state legislatures, and city and county councils are elected representatives of the citizens. These legislative branches are responsible for overseeing the activities of the executive branch. The executive branch reports to the legislative branch concerning financial matters. A budget is presented to the legislative branch for approval. The legislators are responsible for approving tax rates and for maintaining the fiscal viability of the government.

Many of the accounting and financial reporting practices that are peculiar to governmental organizations result from the strong **oversight responsibility** that the legislative branch has over the executive branch in financial matters. Budgetary accounting, fund accounting, encumbrances, modified accrual accounting, and similar practices originated from the oversight process. These practices provide a means for the legislators to control the financial operations of the executive and the departments which are managed by the executive branch.

Oversight groups are primary users of governmental and nonprofit accounting information. These groups are responsible to constituents for the financial management of organization resources. They should carefully monitor financial statements to determine compliance with budgets, continued financial viability, and stewardship of resources. These oversight boards are responsible to constituents for seeing that the organization is run efficiently and that resources are obtained and used judiciously.

The detailed information that is reported on a fund basis by governments and nonprofit organizations provides information to the legislative or oversight group concerning how resources have been obtained, how they have been used, and whether the sources and uses conform to budget requirements. Resources that are restricted to be used for specific purposes are reported separately from other resources so that their use can be monitored.

Many of the disclosures that are part of governmental and nonprofit financial reports provide information about whether the organization has complied with externally imposed financial requirements. These requirements may be imposed by granting agencies, by creditors, by contributors, or directly by the legislative oversight group. Whatever the source of the requirements, the oversight group is, in the final analysis, responsible for seeing that the requirements have been met. The oversight group is politically, legally, and (in some cases) financially responsible to those who elected them. If they fail to meet these responsibilities, they are subject to not being reelected as well as to civil and criminal penalties. Accordingly, the financial reports of governmental and nonprofit organizations are tailored to the information needs of the legislative oversight groups.

The decisions made by oversight groups are broader than those of creditors and grantors. The groups are concerned with service availability both in the short run and in the long run, with determining which services will be provided, and with seeing that current and long-term obligations are met. Also, they are concerned with seeing that grant requirements are met and that grants are solicited when eligibility requirements are met, with seeing that services and costs are distributed equitably, and with seeing that physical resources are properly maintained. Many of these decisions involve the use of financial information.

Financial ratios can be compared over time or to ratios of other similar organizations to determine management efficiency. An examination of expenditures by function and a comparison of actual to budgeted amounts can be used to assess compliance. The fiscal viability of an organization can be assessed by using ratios similar to those discussed earlier in this chapter. For example, the Government Finance Officers Association has outlined a set of financial data

items that city or county council members might consider in evaluating potential financial difficulties.[4] These include:

1 An increase in the percent of expenditures for basic services that are
funded by intergovernmental revenues
2 An increase in the portion of nonintergovernmental revenues being used
to meet matching fund requirements
3 An increase in debt burden
4 Consistent budget overruns in specific funds, departments, or programs
5 A rapid increase in employee fringe benefits
6 Tax rates that are approaching legal limits
7 An increase in per capita expenditures, adjusted for inflation
8 Operating losses in enterprises
9 Short-term debt outstanding at year-end
10 Use of long-term debt for operating purposes
11 Funding for fixed assets declining
12 An increase in the deferral of current pension costs
13 An increase in the interest cost of debt
14 An increase in the difference between actual and budgeted revenues
15 An increase in the amount of uncollected taxes and fees

Other information has been suggested for analyzing the financial management of governmental and nonprofit organizations.[5] Some of these recommended items and their interpretations are provided in Exhibit 3-3.

INFORMATION NEEDS OF CONSTITUENTS

Taxpayers, members, contributors, and service recipients are the constituents
of governmental and nonprofit organizations. These constituents are concerned about the availability of desired services and the cost of a satisfactory
level of services. In most cases, information about the quality and quantity of
services and about direct costs is readily apparent to constituents from the services they receive and the amounts they pay for membership fees or taxes. It
is not necessary to read financial reports to get this information. Constituents
have few incentives to obtain or use financial information unless there is some
direct payoff. However, constituents recognize that managers of governmental
and nonprofit resources will not always use those resources to maximize the
welfare of the constituents unless some oversight is provided. Thus, constituents choose boards of directors or councils to oversee management behavior
as discussed in the previous section.

Since constituents are concerned with services and costs, the information

---

[4]GFOA, "Is Your City Heading for Financial Difficulty?" 1978.
[5]For further discussion see J. Aronson, *Municipal Fiscal Indicators,* Urban Consortium, 1980,
and S. Groves, *Financial Trend Monitoring System,* International City Management Association,
1980.

EXHIBIT 3-3

INFORMATION FOR ANALYSIS OF NONPROFIT FINANCIAL MANAGEMENT

Item	Significance
Excess of expendable assets over liabilities (fund balance), and this excess related to expenses; levels of income-producing assets	Extent to which organization has a reserve against hard times and/or the ability to expand to take advantage of new opportunities
Liquid assets (cash and marketable securities) related to near-term cash needs (current liabilities and ongoing expenses)	Ability of organization to meet its obligations as they come due
Levels of receivables, inventory, and other less productive assets	Extent to which organization has allowed its resources to be tied up in these assets
Comparison of key data to similar data in prior periods (cash, total assets, fund balances, other data appropriate to organization)	Whether organization is better or worse off than it was before
Excess of revenue over expenses	Whether organization is both living within its means and maximizing use of its resources
Comparison of actual to budgeted data, and explanation of differences	Extent to which the organization engages in realistic planning and adequate financial control
Ratio of program expenses to total expenses	Extent to which organization uses its resources for direct community benefit
Ratio of fund raising costs to contributions	Efficiency of organization in raising money
Ratio of fees for service received from clients (customers, patrons, students, or other users of services), to costs of providing client services	Extent to which client services are subsidized from other revenue sources
Investment yield	Effectiveness of investment management, and degree of risk assumed by organization
Ratio of "soft" revenue (contributions, grants) to total expenses	Extent to which organization's operations are dependent on revenue which is less certain of being received
Ratio of debt to total assets	Extent to which organization has depended on borrowed resources to finance its operations

needs of creditors and grantors are important to constituents. If information is not available to these resource providers and if the organization is not managed well, outside resources will be more difficult to obtain and will be more costly. Without these external resources, constituents will have to pay more for their services, and the quantity and quality of services will be less than if the resources were available. Accordingly, all of the information needs and decision processes we have discussed for creditors and grantors become part of the information needs and decision processes of constituents and oversight groups.

In addition to the information used in the decisions made by creditors, granting agencies, and oversight groups, constituents may make other uses of financial information. Taxpayers and businesses make decisions about where to reside or operate, which organizations to join or support, and which services to purchase. Explicitly or implicitly, most of these decisions involve comparisons across locations or organizations. The movements of populations and businesses from one location to another are due, in part, to different levels of services and tax rates in the locations. While these decisions do not always involve a direct examination of financial reports, decisions by major companies and certain individual decisions about location or donations to nonprofit organizations often involve a consideration of financial information. These users are interested in determining the costs of relocating or in knowing how their donations will be used. Information about tax rates and expenditures can be useful in these decisions.

The costs of a thorough analysis of financial information can be high to individual constituents. A considerable amount of time and effort may be needed to digest the data and to make comparisons that are needed for decisions. Since a constituent has only one vote in an election and relatively little direct ability to affect organization decisions, the incentives to expend the time and effort to analyze the information are small. Therefore, it is probably not the case that individual constituents are major users of financial information. Instead, they elect representatives to provide this service for them. In addition, constituents often become members of special interest groups in an effort to develop sufficient political power to affect election or decision outcomes.

In most cases these **special interest groups** develop because of similar views held by their members. Political parties are made up of individuals with similar political philosophies about how resources should be obtained and used. Other interest groups develop because the members have similar economic or geographic interests, for example, employment in a specific industry.

Special interest groups frequently have sufficient economic resources to hire professional financial analysts who can monitor the financial activities of an organization and summarize the important information for members. It is probably in this manner that most financial information about large nonprofit and governmental organizations filters down to individual constituents.

Regardless of the mechanism, the types of uses and information needs of constituents are similar to those discussed earlier for other users. Information which is provided to meet the needs of the other specific users can provide constituents with information about the resources of an organization, where they were obtained, how they were used, and what the future prospects appear to be.

The specific needs of constituents for summary information that is easy to understand or for information about the specific costs and benefits to certain constituents of governmental and nonprofit organization activities have not been the primary focus of the organizations' financial reports. Relatively little

EXHIBIT 3-4

ITEMS PERCEIVED AS USEFUL BY RESPONDENTS
TO GASB SURVEY

Legal tax limits
Annual surplus or deficit
Fund balance available for future appropriation
Accounting standards stressing consistency in reporting over time
Future debt service requirements
Tax-base trend data
Tax collection rates
Tax rates
Description of budgetary procedures and policies
Nonrecurring revenues and expenditures
Accounting standards for comparability across governments
Fund-based financial statements
Schedule of outstanding bonds
Factors giving rise to long-term liabilities
Legal debt limits and unused debt margins
Socioeconomic trend data
Yearly changes in general obligation debt
Total debt authorized
Tax structure data
Tax burden as percent of income
Comparison of budgeted and actual results
Explanation of significant budget amendments
Reconciliation of GAAP to budget basis of accounting
Disclosure of material over- and underexpenditures
Explanation of timing of revenues and expenditures
Designated and undesignated fund balances
Compliance with revenue bond debt service requirements
Future debt service schedules
Independent auditor management letter
Subsidies between general and enterprise funds
Obligations of special public authorities
Schedule of expenditures and revenues by source and function
Modified accrual basis for governmental funds

is known about these information needs, although in recent years the GASB has begun to sponsor research to examine some of these issues for the constituents of state and local governments.

SUMMARY

Financial report analysis is a complex process. This chapter provides a summary of the types of information users obtain from governmental and nonprofit financial reports and a summary of how this information can be used in different decision contexts.

The discussion has not been exhaustive. Other users and uses of governmental and nonprofit financial information can be identified. Employees and vendors are examples. However, the discussion should be sufficient to establish that financial reports are useful and that the content and format of the reports are important.

Standards governing the content and format of financial reports are revised over time. Various organizations are concerned with constructing reports that are more useful to decision makers than current reports or with making sure that current reports provide the information needed by decision makers.

For example, the GASB surveyed various user groups in 1985 to identify the information these groups perceived to be useful.[6] The items reported in Exhibit 3-4 were those perceived to be useful by at least 70 percent of the total respondents to the survey. This and other similar research provides added insight into the uses of governmental and nonprofit financial information. Changes in accounting and reporting for governmental and nonprofit organizations will result from these insights.

A CASE STUDY

Exhibit 3-5 provides comparative information for two cities over a two-year period. How would you describe the financial conditions of these cities relative to each other?

EXHIBIT 3-5
COMPARATIVE ANALYSIS OF ACCOUNTING NUMBERS
(ALL NUMBERS IN THOUSANDS)

	City A		City B	
	19X0	**19X1**	**19X0**	**19X1**
Population	120	110	80	85
Revenues:				
Total operating	$12,600	$12,100	$9,800	$10,300
Restricted	4,200	4,000	2,200	2,300
Intergovernmental	3,400	3,700	1,800	1,900
Nonrecurring	1,300	1,500	600	650
Budgeted operating	12,800	12,500	9,700	10,100
Expenditures:				
Total operating	12,800	12,400	9,650	10,000
Discretionary	3,100	2,700	3,300	3,600
Unrestricted general fund balance	700	400	1,300	1,600
Cash and short-term investments	850	700	2,350	2,600
Current liabilities	1,500	1,800	1,900	2,000
Long-term debt	5,400	6,000	3,200	3,000
Debt service	1,400	1,500	700	650
Unfunded pension liabilities	2,100	2,200	400	300

[6]D. Jones, R. Scott, L. Kimbro, and R. Ingram, *The Needs of Users of Governmental Financial Reports,* GASB, 1985.

First let us examine several financial ratios that can be computed from this information.

1 The general operating revenues per capita for the two cities for the two years are

	City A	City B
19X0	$105.0	$122.5
19X1	110.0	121.2

These ratios demonstrate that revenues are at a higher level on a per capita basis for City B but are growing at a faster rate per capita for City A. A long-term decline in revenues would be a cause for concern.

2 The amounts of restricted, intergovernmental, and nonrecurring revenues as percentages of total revenues are

		City A, %	City B, %
19X0	Restricted	33.3	22.4
	Intergovernmental	27.0	18.4
	Nonrecurring	10.3	6.1
19X1	Restricted	33.1	22.3
	Intergovernmental	30.6	18.4
	Nonrecurring	12.4	6.3

Restricted, intergovernmental, and nonrecurring revenues can be troublesome since frequently they cannot be used to pay for necessary services on an ongoing basis. The relative amounts of these revenues are higher for City A than for City B and are growing, while those for City B are remaining stable. Over 70 percent of the total operating revenues for City A come from these sources.

3 The ratio of actual to budgeted revenues for each city is

	City A	City B
19X0	0.984	1.01
19X1	0.968	1.02

City A is receiving less revenues than budgeted while City B is receiving more. In addition, City A's budget problem appears to be getting worse.

4 The ratio of total operating expenditures to total operating revenues for each city is

	City A	City B
19X0	1.02	0.985
19X1	1.02	0.971

City A is spending more than it is receiving in revenues while City B is spending less.

5 The ratio of discretionary expenditures to total expenditures for each city is

	City A	City B
19X0	0.242	0.342
19X1	0.218	0.360

City A's discretionary expenditures are a smaller portion of total expenditures than are City B's and are decreasing while those for City B are increasing.

6 The ratio of general fund balance to total revenues is

	City A	City B
19X0	0.056	0.133
19X1	0.033	0.155

City A's balance is smaller and declining relative to City B. City A has not generated excesses of revenues over expenditures at the rate of City B.

7 The ratio of cash and short-term investments to current liabilities for each city is

	City A	City B
19X0	0.567	1.24
19X1	0.389	1.30

City B's liquidity is considerably better than that of City A. City A appears to be headed for difficulty in paying current obligations as they become due.

8 The ratios of long-term debt revenues, debt services to revenues, and unfunded pension liabilities to revenues are

		City A	City B
19X0	Long-term debt	0.429	0.327
	Debt service	0.111	0.071
	Unfunded pension liabilities	0.167	0.041
19X1	Long-term debt	0.496	0.291
	Debt service	0.124	0.063
	Unfunded pension liabilities	0.182	0.029

These ratios are larger for City A and are increasing, while those for City B are decreasing.

From these ratios, it is apparent that City B has a stronger financial condition and lower default risk than City A. The ratios do not tell us whether either city is facing a major financial crisis. However, City A does appear to be on a course that will eventually lead to major problems.

Two years of data are inadequate for drawing conclusions about long-range prospects. On the other hand, a number of red flags have been raised about City A that should lead creditors, managers, council members, and taxpayers to investigate the causes of the financial conditions.

KEY CONCEPTS AND TERMS

Creditors
Default risk
General revenues
General obligation bonds
Revenue bonds
Financial ratios
Bond ratings
Debt service
Debt service capacity
Stability of revenue sources
Sinking funds
Liquidity

Demographic and socioeconomic
   attributes
Overlapping debt
Legal debt limits
Taxing capacity
Discretionary expenditures
Nondiscretionary expenditures
Unfunded liabilities
Market risk
Third-party provider
Oversight responsibility
Special interest groups

APPENDIX 3: Auditing Governmental and Nonprofit Organizations

GOVERNMENTAL ORGANIZATIONS

The governmental audit environment is different from that of business in several ways. A business obtains an audit for a financial report on its financial position, results of operations, and cash flows. This type of audit is a financial audit. A government may obtain an audit for many different reasons and for different users. A financial audit report may be required by the governing board, citizens, creditors, and rating agencies. A compliance audit report may be required for certain restricted resources such as federal grants. A performance audit report may be requested by citizens or others to determine if resources provided were utilized in the most economical and efficient manner to provide the desired services. The three basic types of governmental audits are financial, compliance, and performance.

A financial audit examines whether financial reports are prepared in accordance with generally accepted accounting principles (GAAP) such as GASB and FASB pronouncements. An independent accountant must render an opinion as to whether the financial statements are fairly presented in accordance with GAAP.

Many governments were not routinely obtaining financial audits until federal revenue-sharing legislation was enacted in 1975 that required an audit in accordance with GAAP at least every three years for recipients of $100,000 or more of federal funds. This "once every three year" audit requirement was changed to an annual requirement effective in 1980. Federal revenue sharing was eliminated but many governments continued to obtain audits for other reasons. Rating agencies such as Standard & Poor's and Moody's also required GAAP audits for rating requests on long-term obligations.

The Single Audit Act of 1984 was enacted to require any state or local government receiving more than $100,000 in federal funding to obtain a "single audit" for federal purposes. Each grant had been audited individually for compliance purposes prior to the single audit act. The intent of the single audit act was to reduce duplication of audits and to ensure adequate audit coverage of all federal funds. Each government was to obtain one audit to determine compliance with program requirements for all federal funds and grants received.

In response to the single audit requirement, additional professional guidance was developed to aid auditors engaged for this type of audit. The "yellow book," *Government Auditing Standards*,[7] established standards for conduct of audits of governmental entities. The standards include generally accepted auditing standards (GAAS) such as planning and supervision, internal controls, and evidential matter for field work and GAAP compliance, consistency, disclosures, and opinions for reporting standards. The yellow book expands GAAS to require additional field work and reporting standards. The three types of audits (financial, compliance, and performance) are explained. General standards for governmental audits include qualifications, independence, due professional care, and quality control. The yellow book establishes GAGAS, generally accepted governmental auditing standards, which include general standards as well as field work and reporting standards for both financial and performance audits.

The American Institute of Certified Public Accountants (AICPA) issued *Statement on Auditing Standards No. 63*[8] (SAS 63) to provide additional guidance to CPAs conducting a single audit. SAS 63 provides specific guidance on compliance testing as it relates to conducting a single audit for compliance with federal programs. The AICPA also issued an audit guide[9] to aid CPAs conducting governmental financial audits.

The governmental audit environment requires a different approach and techniques to that required for financial audits of businesses. Auditors must have an understanding of the governmental environment, GAAP for governmental units, and GAGAS to effectively conduct an audit for governmental clients.

---

[7]*Government Auditing Standards*, United States General Accounting Office, Washington, D.C., 1988.

[8]*Statement on Auditing Standards No. 63*, "Compliance Auditing Applicable to Governmental Entities and Other Recipients of Governmental Financial Assistance," AICPA, New York, 1989.

[9]*Audits of State and Local Governmental Units*, Audit and Accounting Guide, AICPA, New York, 1986.

NONPROFIT ORGANIZATIONS

The nonprofit audit environment more closely parallels the business audit environment in that the primary emphasis is on financial auditing. However, the emphasis differs in its focus on services provided in relation to the organization's objectives. Another important focus is on the correct utilization of resources for restricted purposes either by donors or grantees. Financial and compliance audits are the primary types of audits conducted, but performance audits also may be utilized when appropriate.

The AICPA has separate industry audit guides for each of the four categories of nonprofit organizations: colleges and universities, hospitals, voluntary health and welfare, and other nonprofit organizations.[10] These audit guides provide general background information on accounting requirements and treatment of common revenue and expense items as well as sample financial statements.

The single audit requirement for state and local governments has been extended to include nonprofit organizations with the issuance of OMB (Office of Management and the Budget) Circular A-133[11] effective for fiscal years beginning after January 1, 1990. Circular A-133 requires a single audit at least every two years for all nonprofit institutions that receive over $100,000 in federal funds. Nonprofit institutions are defined to include all nonprofit organizations, including institutions of higher education, except hospitals, unless they are affiliated with an institution of higher education or an Indian tribe.

The auditor commencing an audit of a nonprofit organization should have an appreciation of the unique fund accounting structure and service focus of these organizations. The auditor should consult professional references for appropriate guidance.

DISCUSSION QUESTIONS

1 Identify the major users of governmental and nonprofit financial reports and the types of decisions these users make that involve the use of financial information.
2 What is default risk? How can default risk be measured? What effect does default risk have on bond prices?
3 How does the concept of intergenerational equity affect the use of long-term debt by governmental organizations?
4 How do general obligation bonds differ from revenue bonds?
5 How does fund accounting by governmental and nonprofit organizations assist creditors in making decisions?
6 What is debt service? What is debt service capacity?

---

[10]Industry Audit Guide, AICPA, New York: (a) *Audits of Colleges and Universities,* Committee on College and University Accounting and Auditing, 2d ed., 1975. (b) *Hospital Audit Guide,* Subcommittee on Health Care Matters, 6th ed., 1985. (c) *Audits of Voluntary Health and Welfare Organizations,* 2d ed., 1988. (d) *Audits of Certain Nonprofit Organizations,* Subcommittee on Nonprofit Organizations, 2d ed., 1987.

[11]OMB Circular A-133, "Audits of Institutions of Higher Education and Other Nonprofit Institutions," March 16, 1990.

7 How is revenue stability important in assessing the default risk of revenue bonds?

8 What are reserve funds? How is information about reserve funds used by creditors?

9 Why are general fund revenues an important measure for determining the general obligation debt capacity of a government?

10 What is the legal debt limit of a government? How is this limit used in assessing a government's debt capacity?

11 Why are some general revenue sources better protection against default risk than others?

12 What risks are associated with the use of intergovernmental revenues by a government?

13 What are discretionary expenditures? How are they relevant for assessing a government's default risk?

14 Why is having short-term debt outstanding at fiscal year-end a signal of financial stress?

15 How is information about postretirement benefits relevant for creditor decisions?

16 What is market risk? How does it affect creditor decisions?

17 In what two ways is accounting information useful to organizations which provide grants to nonprofit organizations?

18 How is fund accounting relevant to accounting for grants?

19 How does compliance associated with grants affect accounting by governmental and nonprofit organizations?

20 How is the relationship between actual and budgeted revenues and expenditures useful information? Who uses this information?

21 What role do boards of directors play for governmental and nonprofit organizations? Who is on the board of directors of a local government?

22 In what ways is governmental and nonprofit accounting structured to meet the needs of oversight groups?

23 Why are individual constituents often not primary users of governmental and nonprofit financial information? In what ways are constituents likely to make use of this information?

PROBLEMS

1 Two nonprofit organizations are considering issuing long-term bonds. Each organization wishes to issue $300,000 of bonds in order to expand physical structures. The minimum interest rate on the bonds would be 8 percent. The excess of revenues over expenses for the two organizations for the last five years is provided below. The earnings of each organization would probably increase by 10 percent annually, on average, as a result. Which organization appears to have a higher default risk? Why?

| | Organization | |
Year	A	B
19X0	$30,000	$70,000
19X1	70,000	63,000
19X2	96,000	75,000
19X3	40,000	68,000
19X4	84,000	77,000

2 The general fund revenues and expenditures for two cities are summarized below. Which city is likely to have the higher default risk for general obligation bonds? Why?

	City			
	A		B	
	19X1	19X0	19X1	19X0
Revenues:				
Restricted	$ 250,000	$ 220,000	$ 85,000	$ 91,000
Intergovernmental	475,000	496,000	78,000	74,000
Other	637,000	622,000	246,000	230,000
Total revenues	$1,362,000	$1,338,000	$409,000	$395,000
Expenditures:				
Discretionary	$ 320,000	$ 315,000	$175,000	$168,000
Nondiscretionary	849,000	860,000	220,000	212,000
Total expenditures	$1,169,000	$1,175,000	$395,000	$380,000

3 The amounts of long-term debt issued and expenditures for fixed assets for the past five years are reported below for two cities. From your examination of this information, which city appears to be experiencing the greater financial stress? Explain your answer.

	City A		City B	
Year	Debt	Fixed Assets	Debt	Fixed Assets
19X1	$ 850,000	$840,000	$2,200,000	$2,100,000
19X2	600,000	610,000	2,000,000	2,100,000
19X3	720,000	680,000	1,500,000	1,480,000
19X4	1,030,000	930,000	2,500,000	2,475,000
19X5	910,000	800,000	2,000,000	2,050,000

4 From the information provided below, compute the following ratios for each organization: (a) current ratio, (b) times interest earned, (c) accounts receivable turnover, (d) return on investment. Compare the financial conditions of the two organizations in light of these ratios.

Measure	Organization A	Organization B
Current assets	$240,000	$ 600,000
Accounts receivable, average net	60,000	80,000
Total assets	500,000	1,000,000
Current liabilities	200,000	410,000
Net service revenue	300,000	970,000
Interest expense	50,000	87,000
Net income	10,000	140,000
Equity	70,000	280,000

5 Compute the annual debt service for the organization reported below. Based on this information, what can you say about its debt capacity?

	Debt payments		
Year	Interest	Principal	Net income
19X1	$100,000	$ 75,000	$260,000
19X2	120,000	100,000	250,000
19X3	150,000	125,000	275,000

6 Information is provided below for the West County Electric Utility. The average for each measure is provided for other electric utilities in the same geographic area. How would you evaluate West County Electric Utility's financial condition?

Measure	West County	Average
Rate per hour	$.12	$.08
Accounts receivable	$ 80,000	$ 110,000
Current assets	200,000	300,000
Total assets	890,000	1,400,000
Current liabilities	175,000	220,000
Long-term debt	680,000	750,000
Equity	35,000	430,000
Interest expense	70,000	70,000
Net sales	650,000	800,000
Net income	140,000	250,000

7 Evaluate the relative financial conditions of the two cities described below. Which city is likely to have the higher default risk on its general obligation debt?

Measure	City A	City B
Population, 19X0	3,000	6,200
Population, 19X1	3,050	6,000
Total general revenue, 19X0	$ 2,600,000	$ 7,500,000
Total general revenue, 19X1	2,950,000	7,460,000
Total general obligation debt, 19X0	6,800,000	23,000,000
Total general obligation debt, 19X1	7,000,000	26,000,000
Legal debt limit	15,000,000	30,000,000
Intergovernmental revenues, 19X0	90,000	1,100,000
Intergovernmental revenues, 19X1	110,000	1,150,000
Total general expenditures, 19X0	2,580,000	7,490,000
Total general expenditures, 19X1	2,945,000	7,485,000

8 The following information describes changes in certain financial data for High City over the last four years. What do these changes indicate about High City's financial condition?

Measure	19X1	19X2	19X3	19X4
Total general revenue	$6,500	$ 6,450	$ 6,610	$ 6,820
Total general obligation debt	9,800	10,000	10,000	10,000
Interest expense	500	510	510	510
Principal payments	1,000	1,000	1,000	1,000
Property tax revenue	3,200	3,250	3,260	3,265

9 Information relative to the general funds of two governments is provided below. Compare the relative financial conditions of the two governments.

Measure	Government A	Government B
Total assessed value of property	$100,295,000	$216,312,000
Total market value of property	175,680,000	230,540,000
Total property tax revenue	601,770	1,946,808
Total property tax collected	598,825	1,786,200
Total expenditures	1,130,275	3,200,112
Discretionary expenditures	362,904	426,711
Total revenues	1,132,560	3,197,880
Short-term debt, end of year	10,000	250,000
General fund balance	270,600	(392,100)

10 Information about the operations of two health care facilities is provided below. Calculate the following ratios for each organization: (a) current ratio, (b) days in patient accounts receivable, (c) average payment period ratio, (d) days cash on hand, (e) equity financing ratio, (f) fixed asset financing ratio, (g) times interest earned, (h) operating margin ratio, (i) return on assets. Describe the relative financial conditions of the two organizations.

Measure	Facility A	Facility B
Current assets	$ 420,000	$ 375,000
Patient accounts receivable	210,000	142,000
Cash and marketable securities	80,000	59,000
Net fixed assets	5,470,000	4,890,000
Total assets	6,235,000	5,782,000
Current liabilities	386,000	291,000
Long-term debt	3,720,000	3,496,000
Net patient service revenue	1,310,000	1,164,000
Operating revenue	1,365,000	1,212,000
Operating expenses	1,162,000	1,034,000
Depreciation expense	369,000	326,000
Interest expense	350,000	344,000
Total revenue	1,420,000	1,306,000
Total expenses	1,265,000	1,159,000

11 The City of South Hill has received a grant from the state government to provide street improvements. The grant is restricted to this one purpose and all grant money must be used or encumbered by the end of the current year. The City will be reimbursed for all expenditures made under the terms of the grant. Discuss the accounting procedures that South Hill could use to ensure compliance with the conditions of the grant and to ensure proper reimbursement of expenditures.

12 You have been elected to the elected to the East Valley City Council. One of your tasks is to oversee the expenditures made by the City government. You received the following report from one department of the City government. What accounting problems are apparent in the report? How could the report be modified to make it more useful to you? As a citizen of East Valley, what other information might be useful to you concerning the operations of the department?

Department A
Statement of Revenues and Expenditures
For the Year Ended June 30, 19X0

Revenues...		$1,600,000
Expenditures:		
Salaries and benefits.............................	$850,000	
Supplies and equipment	390,000	
Other operating	240,000	
Fixed assets......................................	100,000	1,580,000
Excess of revenues over expenditures.........................		$ 20,000

4

Understanding the Basic Accounting Cycle

The previous chapters introduced the accounting concepts and financial reports for governmental and nonprofit organizations and compared them with those of business organizations. These chapters were oriented toward developing a general understanding of governmental and nonprofit financial reports. Therefore, attention was given to the content of these reports and how the content could be used by decision makers. Chapters 4 and 5 provide more detailed discussions of processing and disclosure of financial transactions in governmental and nonprofit organizations. The objective of Chapter 4 is to describe the transactions and procedures that lead to governmental financial reports and to describe the accounting treatment of basic transactions that frequently occur in governmental organizations. Chapter 5 will describe more complex transactions that may be observed in governmental organizations and will consider certain transactions of nonprofit organizations. First, we will look at the typical accounting cycle in governmental units.

THE BUDGETARY CYCLE

As we have stressed in earlier chapters, governmental funds have a spending and measurement focus; that is, the emphasis is on accounting for operations within the current budgetary year. Characteristics of such transactions for the governmental funds will be illustrated in this chapter. These transactions will appear in the general fund (or in a special revenue fund if specific budgetary control is required). The transactions described in this chapter may occur in the capital projects fund as well, although the initial appropriation or project authorization is often recorded by only a "memo" entry in this fund. The debt service fund does not use budgetary accounts since it only expends resources for debt service.

The actual amount by which a budget is over- or underspent each year is added or subtracted to the Fund Balance through closing journal entries. A positive Fund Balance is represented by a credit balance. The resources represented by a Fund Balance may be reserved for specific purposes such as en-cumbrances (purchase orders) outstanding. The fund balance which is not des-ignated is called **Unreserved Fund Balance.**

Exhibit 4-1 illustrates the budgetary cycle and summarizes the sequence of major financial and budgetary events recorded in a governmental fund. To read Exhibit 4-1, start at "Record appropriations" and read clockwise to "Fis-cal Year-End." Reference to this exhibit will enhance understanding of the fol-lowing discussion about accounting for the general fund.

BUDGETARY ACCOUNTS AND ACCOUNTING PROCEDURES

Budgetary account balances are established at the beginning of a fiscal year by journal entries to record the legislative body's appropriation act or ordinance that authorizes the use of financial resources. These budgetary accounts are closed at fiscal year-end to the Unreserved Fund Balance. The budgetary ac-counts reflect one unique feature of governmental accounting which reflects the importance of legal authorization and accountability for the accounting

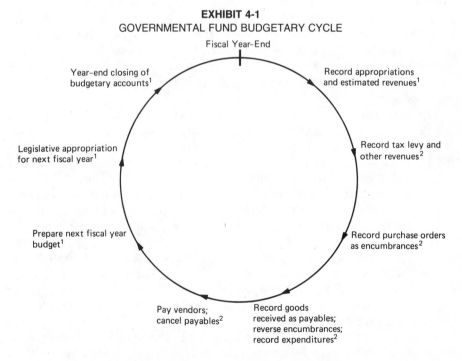

EXHIBIT 4-1
GOVERNMENTAL FUND BUDGETARY CYCLE

Fiscal Year-End

Year-end closing of budgetary accounts[1]

Record appropriations and estimated revenues[1]

Legislative appropriation for next fiscal year[1]

Record tax levy and other revenues[2]

Prepare next fiscal year budget[1]

Record purchase orders as encumbrances[2]

Pay vendors; cancel payables[2]

Record goods received as payables; reverse encumbrances; record expenditures[2]

[1] One-time events—appropriations and estimated revenues may be revised throughout the fiscal year.

[2] Transactions recur throughout the budgetary cycle.

system of a government entity. The political and legal environment of government has a profound influence on the accounting procedures.

Let's refer to the example of the City of East River to illustrate budgetary accounting procedures. The reader should recall that the City Council hired a manager to oversee day-to-day operations of the City. The budgetary accounts provide a means for the City Council to monitor whether or not the manager is expending funds within the authority provided by the City Council. Generally, by midyear the manager would present a budget request to the City Council for the next fiscal year. This budget request would have been developed from estimates of the cost of various service functions and estimates of the amounts of various sources of revenues expected by the public sector organization. After the City Council has reviewed the budget, they make any desired adjustments and enact appropriations for the next fiscal year. This approved document will govern the spending authority of the city mayor or manager (and department managers in large public sector organizations) for the next fiscal year and will determine how anticipated revenues will be allocated among services that are provided. At the beginning of the fiscal year, Appropriations and Estimated Revenues are recorded. **Appropriations** reflect how much the City Council, through the budget, is permitting the government to expend for various functions and services. **Estimated Revenues** reflect how much money the City Council expects to receive from taxes, fees, and certain other revenue sources. Estimated Other Financing Sources reflect how much money the City Council expects to receive from nonrecurring sources such as long-term debt issuance or sale of fixed assets. **Estimated Other Financing Sources** and **Estimated Other Financing Uses** are budgetary accounts which reflect the inflow and outflow of financial resources which do not meet the definition of revenues and expenditures.

Revenues result from inflows of financial resources that increase the net resources of the governmental unit. Expenditures result from net decreases in resources from the outflow of financial resources. Financial flows from the issuance of debt or sale of fixed assets increase the current financial resources available to a governmental fund. On the other hand, they do not increase the total equity of the governmental unit, just as they are not revenues or expenses of business organizations. Financial resources received from issuing debt must be repaid, and prior expenditures were made for fixed assets which are sold during the current period. Other types of financing sources and uses include interfund transfers. **Operating Transfers Out** are transfers of cash from a fund receiving revenue (usually the general fund) to a fund authorized to expend resources for specific purposes (for example, a capital projects fund). **Operating Transfers In** are recorded by the receiving fund.

Estimated Other Financing Sources are used in recording the budget if the government expects significant resources within this category which will be appropriated for use. If you recall the statement of revenues, expenditures, and changes in fund balance explained in Chapter 2, you will note that Other Financing Sources (Uses) appear after expenditures are subtracted from revenues to arrive at excess of revenues over expenditures. This segregation of Other Financing Sources (Uses) in the financial report is intended to prevent readers from confusing ordinary operating activities that are likely to reoccur on a regular basis with nonoperating activities and with those activities that are not likely to reoccur on a regular basis.

The difference between the sum of Appropriations and Estimated Other Financing Uses and the sum of Estimated Revenues and Estimated Other Financing Sources represents the net amount of financial resources that the governmental unit expects to spend or receive during the year. These budgetary accounts indicate whether the government expects to receive more financial resources than will be expended during the year. A governmental unit expecting to expend more resources than it expects to receive must plan in advance to reduce its Unreserved Fund Balance or to borrow. Similarly, a governmental unit expecting to receive more money than it plans to spend will have an excess of resources to carry forward to future budget periods.

As we have emphasized earlier, governments often have legal constraints on borrowing to finance deficit-spending. When such constraints exist and a deficit is expected, they must reduce planned expenditures so that they do not exceed legally available resources. Therefore, budgetary accounting is an important tool to assist the City Council of East River to manage planned expenditures and to monitor expenditures to see that they comply with the budget. An important feature of budgetary accounting is that it also provides a basis for making adjustments to the planned expenditures (budget) on a timely basis if the financial condition of a government changes (for example, revenues are higher or lower than estimated).

Suppose that the proposed budget for the City of East River for the fiscal year beginning January 1, 19X1, is as follows:

Estimated revenues:	
Property taxes	$1,800,000
Sales taxes	400,000
Total	$2,200,000
Other financing sources	150,000
Total	$2,350,000
Appropriations:	
Education	$ 900,000
Police and fire protection	750,000
Streets and sanitation	350,000
General administration	300,000
Total	$2,300,000

The budget would have been approved by the elected City Council prior to January 1, 19X1. As discussed above, the Council appropriates (provides the legal authority to spend) funds for operations prior to the beginning of a fiscal year. When a budget is enacted, the manager of the governmental unit may spend no more than is appropriated in each category without obtaining further approval from the Council. Thus, the appropriations are the authorized expenditures that can be made by the government during the fiscal year. The budget can usually be modified during the year if the Council approves of the modifications. In order to gain a conceptual understanding of nonprofit accounting, it is important to remember that government officials may be subject to legal action for expending funds without an appropriation.

The following journal entry would be recorded by the City of East River's accountant as of January 1, 19X1:

Estimated Revenues	2,200,000	
Estimated Other Financing Sources	150,000	
Unreserved Fund Balance		50,000
Appropriations		2,300,000

The debit to Estimated Revenues and the credit to Appropriations create control account balances against which actual revenues and expenditures can be compared during the year. **Subsidiary accounts** for the individual revenue and expenditure categories (for example, property and sales taxes) will be created to provide detailed information on which the totals in the control accounts are based. Separate accounts will be maintained for each appropriation category. If $40,000 of the total education appropriation was for library subscriptions, the Library Subscription Appropriation account would report a credit balance of $40,000 at the beginning of the fiscal year to reflect the authorization for the librarian to expend resources for subscriptions. An example of how such an account might appear after recording the subsidiary information is as follows:

Library Subscriptions

Appropriations	Encumbrances	Expenditures	Balance
40,000	—	—	40,000

When the budget is recorded at the beginning of the fiscal year, the difference between the Estimated Revenues and Other Financing Sources control balance and the Appropriations and Estimated Other Financing Uses control balance is credited to the Unreserved Fund Balance indicating that a surplus of $50,000 ($2,350,000 − $2,300,000) is expected for the fiscal year. Alternately, the estimated surplus can be credited to Budgetary Fund Balance and then closed to Unreserved Fund Balance at fiscal year-end. If this surplus is actually realized, it will be available for use by the City Council in future periods.

It is also possible that Appropriations could be credited for an amount in excess of Estimated Revenues, resulting in an initial debit to the Unreserved Fund Balance. This entry would indicate that a surplus from prior years was expected to be used to finance the anticipated negative impact of operations of the current year.

OPERATING ACCOUNTS AND ACCOUNTING PROCEDURES

In the last section, new accounting procedures were introduced having to do with recording the budget estimates of a governmental unit at the beginning of a budget period. The following material will discuss the accounting practices followed to record actual operating transactions of a governmental unit.

Recording Taxes and Other Revenues

The Revenue accounts reflect actual revenues recorded during the fiscal year. At fiscal year-end these accounts are closed in a manner similar to that followed in business organization accounting. These accounts must be closed periodically in order to measure the operating results of the fund and to provide an accounting mechanism to accumulate periodic transaction data for the next accounting period.

At the conclusion of a budget period, the difference between the Estimated Revenues (budgetary control account) and the Revenues (operating control account) indicates whether the unit received more or less revenues than was projected when the budget was enacted and recorded.

Modified accrual accounting, which currently is used by governmental funds, requires that actual revenues be recorded when the amount of the revenue is "measurable and available." Normally, revenues are determined to be measurable and available when they are legally due to the government and will be received in time to pay expenditures and encumbrances of the current fiscal year. Property taxes are legally due to the government upon levy (billing) to property owners. In general, the revenue recognition criteria will emphasize the underlying transaction and government demand when *Statement No. 11,* "Measurement Focus and Basis of Accounting," takes effect in 1994. Sales tax revenue is accrued when the sale takes place if the government has demanded the taxes regardless of when the cash is received. Income tax revenue should be accrued in the period when the related income is earned by the individual or corporate taxpayer if the government has demanded the taxes regardless of when cash is received. Fines, fees for licenses and permits, and donations should generally be accrued when the underlying event takes place and the government has a legally enforceable claim regardless of when cash is received.

If we assume that for the City of East River all property taxes will be collected before the end of the fiscal year but that 2 percent are estimated to be uncollectible, the 19X1 property tax levy would be recorded as:

Property Taxes Receivable—Current.......... 1,800,000		
Property Taxes Revenue............................	1,764,000	
Allowance for Uncollectible Taxes—Current..........		36,000

In this entry, Property Taxes Receivable-–Current should be viewed as a control account that would be supported by subsidiary accounts which identify and control the amounts due from individual taxpayers.

If $26,000 of property taxes are received during January 19X1, the following entry would be recorded:

General Fund Cash 26,000	
Property Taxes Receivable—Current.....................	26,000

Other forms of tax revenues are generally not recorded until the amounts are received since they are frequently "self-assessed" (the taxpayer determines the amount due), and the timing and amount may not be easily predicted. Sales taxes, fines, parking fees, license fees, and similar revenues are examples of such items that often are not recorded until cash is received. For example, if we assume that the City of East River received $800 in parking fees during January 19X1, the revenue would be recorded as

General Fund Cash 800	
Parking Revenues..	800

Accounting for governmental organizations will change to an accrual basis in 1994.[1] Two factors will be considered in measuring tax revenue: (1) the underlying transaction or event, and (2) the demand for taxes. The demand for taxes will be considered made by the government if a due date occurs on or before the end of the fiscal period. Taxpayer-assessed taxes (sales and income) with a due date within two months after fiscal year end will be considered demanded as of the end of the period.

Tax revenue accruals for delinquent taxes should include amounts taxpayers are late in reporting or remitting. Revenue should be calculated based upon amounts (1) received before financial statements are issued, (2) reported but not received before financial statements are issued, and (3) expected to be reported after financial statements are issued based on historical evidence.

Final settlements expected during or within two months after fiscal year-end are considered current final settlements and should be accrued. Estimated additional payments for future final settlements of income and other taxpayer-assessed taxes should not be recognized as revenues of the current period.

[1]"Measurement Focus and Basis of Accounting—Governmental Fund Operating Statements," *Statement No. 11 of the Governmental Accounting Standards Board,* May 1990.

Investment Transactions

Governmental organizations may have cash in excess of their current operating needs. In such circumstances they may choose to invest in securities for either the short term or the long term. These transactions are recorded in the same manner as they are by business organizations.

Under the assumption that a governmental unit has $300,000 of cash in excess of its current operating financial requirements, the investment of such funds would be recorded as follows:

Investments	300,000	
Cash		300,000

When interest accrues on the investment, an entry would be made to record the earned revenue:

Interest Receivable on Investments	30,000	
Interest Revenue		30,000

The receipt of the accrued interest is recorded:

Cash	30,000	
Interest Receivable on Investments		30,000

When the investment is sold for cash, the following entry properly records the sale of the investment:

Cash	300,000	
Investments		300,000

Any amount of cash received in excess of the original investment or less than the original investment would be recorded as a gain or loss and is closed to the Fund Balance at the end of the current fiscal period.

Residual Equity Transfers

Residual equity transfers occur when one fund transfers equity to another. An example of circumstances which would result in a residual equity transfer would be the general fund contributing equity to start a motor pool (internal service fund). Conversely, a capital projects fund which has completed its purpose might transfer any remaining fund balance to the general fund or debt service fund. For illustration purposes, let's assume that the governmental unit decides to start a motor pool and that the general fund contributes $100,000 in cash to establish equity in the motor pool fund. The general fund would record:

Unreserved Fund Balance............................	100,000	
Cash		100,000

This treatment results in a direct reduction of the Unreserved Fund Balance account, rather than the alternative treatment of debiting a Residual Equity Transfer account (which would appear on the statement of revenues and expenditures). The effect of the simpler procedure of debiting Unreserved Fund Balance is that the transfer does not pass through the income statement. It is not treated as an operating item but as a transfer of equity directly between funds.

Upon receipt of the cash from the general fund, the motor pool (internal service) fund records the equity transfer from the general fund with the following entry:

Cash...	100,000	
Contributed Capital		100,000

The motor pool fund would have a separate line labeled Contributed Capital in the amount of $100,000 in the equity section of its balance sheet as long as the fund exists. A summary of the interfund transactions described above is provided in Exhibit 4-2, item 1.

Interfund Loans and Transfers

In financial statements, short-term loans and obligations between funds are commonly labeled *Due to (Name) Fund* and *Due from (Name) fund*. The need for such an account classification frequently results when the general fund is obligated to pay for some of the operations of other funds. For example, let's suppose that the general fund is obligated to pay for a $50,000 share of a capital project cost. The general fund would record:

Operating Transfer Out.................................	50,000	
Due to Capital Projects Fund..............................		50,000

Similarly, the capital projects fund would record the general fund transfer as follows:

Due from General Fund	50,000	
Operating Transfer In..		50,000

When the cash is transferred, Cash would be debited and Due from General Fund would be credited. Exhibit 4-2, item 2, provides a summary of these interfund transactions.

EXHIBIT 4-2
SUMMARY OF INTERFUND AND ACCOUNT GROUP TRANSACTOINS
[Credits in ( )]

Transaction: Account title	General fund	Debt service fund	Capital projects fund	General fixed asset group	General long-term debt group	Internal service fund
1. Create motor pool:						
Unreserved fund balance	$ 100,000					
Cash	(100,000)					$ 100,000
Contributed Capital						(100,000)
2. Transfer of capital project cost:						
Operating transfer out	50,000					
Due to Capital Projects fund	(50,000)					
Due from General Fund			$ 50,000			
Operating Transfer In			(50,000)			
3. Purchase of general fixed asset:						
Expenditures	400					
Cash	(400)					
Office Equipment				$ 400		
Investment in General Fixed Assets				(400)		
4. Sales of general fixed asset:						
Investment in General Fixed Assets				400		
Office Equipment				(400)		
Cash	50					
Other Financing Source	(50)					
5. Issuance of general obligation debt:						
Cash	300,000					
Other Financing Source	(300,000)					
Amount to Be Provided					$ 300,000	
Bonds Payable					(300,000)	
6. Payment of principal and interest:						
Operating Transfer Out	$ 51,000					
Cash	(51,000)	$ 51,000				
Operating Transfer In		(51,000)				
Amount Available					30,000	
Amount to Be Provided					(30,000)	
Expenditure—Principal		30,000				
Expenditure—Interest		21,000				
Cash		(51,000)				
Bonds Payable					30,000	
Amount Available					(30,000)	

Operating Transfers In and Operating Transfers Out represent the resource flows between funds. These titles are used to distinguish the resource flows from revenues and expenditures which increase or decrease the total financial resources available to the governmental unit. Transfers do not increase or decrease total financial resources; they only shift the resources from one fund to another.

If the cash is provided for a period extending beyond the current fiscal year budget, Advance to (Name) Fund or Advance from (Name) Fund is used instead of Transfer In or Transfer Out. These account titles are used to distinguish short-term from long-term resource transfers on the income statement.

External and Quasi-External Transactions

External transactions in which one entity is not a member of the governmental unit may occur. An example of such a transaction which could occur would be the sale of power by a public power utility (the governmental unit) to a household (the "external" unit). Such a transaction arises because many governments own electric utility companies which sell electricity to customers outside the government. If such a utility also supplies electricity to the governmental unit of which it is a part for a fee (which the general fund or other funds pay), this is considered a **quasi-external transaction.** Quasi-external transactions are accounted for as if the transaction occurred external to the governmental entity; that is, the fund which provides the service would recognize a revenue and the paying fund would recognize an expenditure for this type of transaction.

Intergovernmental Revenue Transactions

Governmental units often receive grants from other governmental units. For example, a city might receive grants from either the state or federal government for the development or maintenance of a project of interest to the state or federal government. Local governments may also receive shared revenues from either the state or federal government. Shared revenues occur when the larger governmental unit returns a portion of taxes it has collected to local governments to be used for local purposes. Both grants and shared revenues result in a similar type of transaction for the governmental unit. If there are no restrictions on the use of the resources, they usually will be recorded in the general fund.

Under the assumption that a city is entitled to receive $400,000, comprising shared revenues from the federal government of $300,000 and shared revenues from the state government of $100,000, the following entry would be appropriate:

Due from State Government	100,000	
Due from Federal Government	300,000	
Revenues		400,000

Similarly, an example of an entry to record receipt of the intergovernmental revenues recognized above is as follows:

Cash..	400,000	
Due from State Government............................		100,000
Due from Federal Government.........................		300,000

These types of transactions result in revenues (or expenditures) rather than transfers since resources are being exchanged between governmental units rather than being exchanged between funds within a governmental unit.

Revenues that are restricted for specific purposes are often recorded in a special revenue fund. For example, federal and state grants for specific purposes are often accounted for by local governments in special revenue funds. If a federal grant were approved for the City of East River for $200,000 to be used for street improvements, the journal entry in the special revenue fund would be:

Grants Receivable—Federal........................	200,000	
Deferred Revenues		200,000

In this situation, the grant proceeds are assumed to be unearned until the conditions of the grant are met; that is, until expenditures are made for the purpose specified by the grant.

Often, actual cash may not be transferred to the receiving government until expenditures for the intended purpose are made. Then, the local government is reimbursed for expenditures approved under conditions of the grant. If $80,000 were spent from the grant, the entries in the special revenue fund would be:

Expenditures	80,000	
Vouchers Payable...		80,000
Deferred Revenues.....................................	80,000	
Revenues		80,000
Cash..	80,000	
Grants Receivable—Federal..............................		80,000
Vouchers Payable	80,000	
Cash		80,000

Accounting for Expenditures and Encumbrances

Since a government cannot spend resources in excess of the amount legally authorized, it must maintain a record of how much it has available to spend in each appropriation category. Organizations normally place orders for goods and services in advance of the receipt of the goods and services. Although purchase orders are not liabilities at the time that an order is placed, they represent an intent to expend resources in the future. For example, the City of East

River may order supplies in advance of actually being billed for these items. If no accounting record of these purchase orders has been maintained, it is possible that the government might overspend its appropriations for supplies leading to serious legal, political, and/or economic consequences for the City of East River Council and for the city management if resources are not available. Even if subsidiary records of such orders are maintained outside the regular accounting records, as would be the case in a business organization, it is still important for the manager and the members of the City Council to have a reliable summary of purchase commitments outstanding, in order to discharge their fiscal duties properly. In business organization accounting, similar purchase orders are frequently issued to suppliers; however, since no liability exists until the order is filled by a supplier, no accounting entry is made at the time that a purchase order is placed.

Therefore, governmental organizations have adopted an accounting procedure which records a purchase order commitment at the time that the purchase order is placed. For example, recall that the City of East River Library was authorized to spend $40,000 for subscriptions in 19X1 and that $38,500 has been spent. Consider the situation which could result if purchase orders for $1,800 of magazine subscriptions were issued but no record had been made of these orders since the bills had not yet been received. The librarian would have authorized expenditure of $40,300 even though the accounting records would only reflect expenditures of $38,500.

To avoid the problem of potential overexpenditures, nonprofit organizations frequently use **encumbrances** to record the expected cost of orders that have been placed but not paid. Thus, when the library ordered subscriptions the following entry would be made in the general fund journal:

Encumbrances—Library Subscriptions 1,200		
Fund Balance Reserved for Encumbrances................1,200		

After this entry is made and posted, the ledger account for library subscriptions would appear as follows:

Library Subscriptions

Appropriations	Expenditures	Encumbrances	Balance
40,000	38,500	1,200	300

One can easily see that by recording the encumbrance, the accounting system provides current control information which encompasses not only actual expenditures but also captures and reports planned future expenditures. Under such a system there is a reduced likelihood that the appropriation will be overexpended because of incomplete accounting information. A simple subtraction of Encumbrances and Expenditures from the Appropriation account will determine the amount in an account which is available for use.

This system of purchase order control requires additional accounting steps when the goods represented by the purchase order are received. At this time, the original encumbrance is reversed since the order has become a legal obligation (liability) of the City of East River. Expenditures are then recorded for the amount of the legal obligation once the goods or services are received. In some cases, the actual price of the good or service purchased may differ from the expected price that was encumbered. For example, although the purchase order was issued for $1,200, the actual library subscription cost may have been only $1,100 because of a discount from the publisher. The following entries provide an example of how this accounting process would occur upon receipt of the invoice to reverse the previous encumbrance and to record the liability for the actual invoice amount:

Fund Balance Reserved for Encumbrances 1,200		
Encumbrances—Library Subscriptions 1,200		
Expenditures—Library Subscriptions......................1,100		
Vouchers Payable...1,100		

The encumbrance is no longer needed since the bill has been received. Therefore, the entry reverses the original encumbrance and records an expenditure for the actual amount of the purchase. Vouchers Payable (or Accounts Payable) is normally credited for amounts that require payment. The following entry will be recorded when the check to pay the liability is issued:

Vouchers Payable 1,100	
General Fund Cash...1,100	

After reversal of the encumbrance and after the expenditure transaction has been recorded, the Library Subscription subsidiary account would appear as follows:

Library Subscriptions

Appropriations	Encumbrances	Expenditures	Balance
40,000	—	39,600	400

Certain types of expenditures do not require that encumbrances be recorded. If payment is made in a relatively short period of time subsequent to a purchase commitment, encumbrances may not be needed. For example, if the City purchased office equipment from a local store for cash, the transaction might be recorded as

Expenditures—Office Equipment.............................400	
General Fund Cash...400	

CLOSING THE ACCOUNTS

Closing entries are made in the accounts of governmental and nonprofit organizations just as they are in businesses in order to summarize the impact of operating transactions on appropriate balance sheet accounts. In the case of a governmental or nonprofit organization, Unreserved Fund Balance will be updated through the closing process in a manner similar to the treatment of retained earnings in a business organization's closing process. Each fund is closed separately at year-end. In a manner similar to practices in business organization accounting, expenditures (expenses) are credited and revenues are debited and the balances are transferred to fund balance.

The closing entries described above serve at least two purposes. One, the operating account and budget account balances are reduced to zero so that the activities of the next fiscal year can be accumulated, and two, the balances of the operating accounts are transferred to the Fund Balance account for each fund, resulting in a measure of the status of the fund at year-end. In addition, the closing process completes the budgetary cycle (Exhibit 4-1) for the current fiscal year so that the correct account balances can be identified for the financial statements of the individual funds.

Since the financial reports require the display of budget, actual, and variance (favorable or unfavorable) amounts, the actual results of the period can now be compared with the budgeted amounts by the City Council or other statement users. Since budgetary accounts were established for governmental funds, these accounts also are closed as part of the closing process. It is customary that actual revenues are closed together with closing entries for Estimated Revenues. Similarly, actual expenditures *and encumbrances* are closed together with appropriations account balances. Each of these closing entries, then, displays in summary fashion the degree to which estimated amounts compare to actual results. The net differences between these budgetary and operating account balances will increase (credit) or decrease (debit) the Unreserved Fund Balance.

If as of December 31, 19X1, the city's actual expenditures were $2,100,000, encumbrances at year-end $100,000, revenues $2,050,000, and other financing sources $150,000, the entries to close the budgetary accounts would be:

Revenues..	2,050,000	
Other Financing Sources.........................	150,000	
Unreserved Fund Balance........................	150,000	
Estimated Revenues......................................		2,200,000
Estimated Other Financing Sources..................		150,000

By choosing to merge related budgetary and operating revenue balances in one closing entry, the accountant is recording the impact on the Fund Balance of differences between actual revenue results and estimates for 19X1. The closing entry for appropriations, expenditures, and encumbrances would be:

Appropriations..................................... 2,300,000		
Expenditures...	2,100,000	
Encumbrances...	100,000	
Unreserved Fund Balance	100,000	

The effect of closing the budgetary and operating accounts is to decrease Unreserved Fund Balance by $150,000 for the amount of underestimation of revenues and to increase it by $100,000 for the amount of underexpended fund resources which results in a net decrease of $50,000 to the Unreserved Fund Balance.

An issue that arises in the closing process for governmental funds is the treatment of supplies. When supplies are purchased, an expenditure is normally recorded in governmental funds to reflect use of the fund's financial resources. If a material amount of supplies remains unused at year-end, a fund asset should be recorded. For example, if $40,000 of supplies are on hand at the end of 19X1, the entry to recognize this asset would be:

Inventory of Supplies..................................... 40,000	
Reserve for Inventory of Supplies 40,000	

The Reserve for Inventory is reported in the Fund Balance section of the balance sheet. During the following fiscal year, this transaction would be reversed to close out the respective account balances, reflecting the use of the supplies. The accounting treatment for prepaid items and supplies will change in 1994 to the accrual basis used by business organizations.

ACCOUNTING FOR ACCOUNT GROUPS

We have previously discussed the legal, political, and economic reasons that governmental funds have a spending and measurement focus that results in a system that accounts only for events which occur during the budgetary cycle. Such systems focus reporting attention on expendable resources rather than on total resources under the management control of the accounting entity. Therefore, no records of fixed assets acquired or long-term debt issued are kept within the governmental funds. However, it is frequently the case that those relying on the information generated by the accounting system will need to know about the total financial obligations or total assets of a governmental entity. In order for users of financial statements to be aware of what is owned and owed after the end of the fiscal period, two account groups, the general fixed asset group and the general long-term debt group, are usually created.

Acquisition and Disposal of General Fixed Assets

Records of fixed assets acquired as well as the sources of the money used to acquire the assets are recorded in the general fixed asset account group. The debit account balances in such an account group represent the cost of assets acquired by the governmental entity. Fixed asset categories normally maintained by local governments include equipment, buildings, improvements other than buildings, and land. The credit account balances within the group reflect summaries of the source of funding used to purchase the assets and are titled **Investment in General Fixed Assets**—(followed by the source). The following sources of funding are commonly found:

Capital project funds:
    General obligation bonds
    Federal grants
    State grants
    Local grants
    Construction in progress
General fund revenues
Special revenue fund revenues
Private gifts
Other sources

Any material expenditure from general revenues that results from the acquisition of an asset that is expected to be in service beyond the current fiscal year should be recorded in the general fixed asset account group in addition to being recorded as an expenditure within the appropriate governmental fund. It is important to note that a single transaction to purchase an asset with a long-term life will impact on the general or other governmental fund and on the general fixed asset account group. The purchase of a typewriter from general fund revenues on July 15, 19X2, would result in the following entries:

General Fund

Expenditures—Office Equipment............................ 400
    Cash.. 400

General Fixed Asset Account Group

Office Equipment—Typewriter................................ 400
    Investment in General Fixed Assets—General
        Fund Revenues 400

Exhibit 4-2, item 3, summarizes this transaction which has a simultaneous effect on the general fund and the general fixed asset account group.

The asset remains in the records of the general fixed asset account group until the city disposes of the asset. Depreciation is not recorded for general fixed assets, although footnote disclosure of depreciation is permitted.

The sale price of long-term assets that are sold is generally recorded as an other financing source in the general fund. For example, if the typewriter is sold after five years for $50, the journal entry for the Account Group would be:

Investment in General Fixed Assets—General Fund
Revenues.. 400
Office Equipment—Typewriter 400

This entry removes the original cost of the item from the Account Group. The corresponding entry in the general fund would be:

General Fund Cash 50
Other Financing Source 50

These interfund transactions are summarized in Exhibit 4-2, item 4.

No attempt is made to measure gains or losses on transactions involving general fixed assets since assets are not maintained in the accounting records at a net of depreciation amount. Also, gains and losses are not of primary importance to governments since governmental organization accounting does not have an income (capital maintenance) focus and since governments do not pay taxes on earnings. Complex transactions such as the construction of fixed assets will be discussed in Chapter 5.

Long-Term Debt Issuance and Payment

Since the accounting focus of the general fund is the current budget period, it is not appropriate to reflect debt obligations of future budget periods in the general fund. Therefore, the governmental funds do not account for their own long-term debt. However, as is the case in accounting for fixed assets, it is frequently true that city councils, managers, and others need a record of future financial obligations which must be repaid. Therefore, such a record of long-term obligations is kept within the general long-term debt account group. In particular, the general long-term debt group should record long-term debt associated with the acquisition of general fixed assets.

Frequently, money received from the issuance of long-term debt is recorded in the general fund. Similarly, payments to retire principal and pay interest are often recorded in the general fund since the source of payment is general fund revenues. Since a separate accounting entity is maintained to record the long-term debt and related interest, entries to issue and retire debt in the governmental funds will normally also require an entry in the general long-term debt account group. Three types of accounts are used in this group. **Amount to Be Provided** reflects how much money is needed in order to pay off an obligation. **Amount Available** reflects how much money is already on hand in a fund (for example, the debt service fund) to pay off an obligation. **Bonds Payable** or a similar liability account is the credit reflecting the principal amount of a long-term liability that will be repaid.

Bonds that are issued to provide financial resources for general government use and that are repaid from general government resources are known as **gen-**

eral obligation bonds. These bonds are recorded in the general long-term debt group. Other bonds are issued to pay for specific projects and are repaid by the revenues earned from these projects (for example, bonds to build a public utility that are repaid from utility revenues). These bonds are known as **revenue bonds** and are recorded in the fund which is responsible for their repayment (usually an enterprise fund).

Issuance of $300,000 in long-term general obligation bonds on July 15, 19X2, would be recorded in the general fund (assuming this fund initially receives the cash) as:

General Fund Cash.................................... 300,000
      Other Financing Sources—Bond Proceeds 300,000

The cash might then be transferred to another fund, such as a capital projects fund, for use. We will examine capital projects funds in more detail in Chapter 5.

The issuance of general obligation bonds would be recorded in the long-term debt account group as:

Amount to Be Provided for Repayment of Long-
    Term Debt.. 300,000
      General Obligation Bonds Payable...................... 300,000

The debit recognizes the amount that will be needed to retire the principal amount which was borrowed. The combined effect of the bond issuance is summarized in Exhibit 4-2, item 5.

General obligation debt generally pledges the "full faith and credit" of the government since general revenues and general government assets are used to secure repayment. A footnote in the financial report should explain any contingent liability of the general fund for obligations of other funds (for example, enterprise funds). These contingent liabilities may become obligations of the general fund if the revenues of the issuing fund are insufficient to meet debt service requirements.

Most general obligation debt is **serial debt**; that is, part of the principal is repaid each fiscal year along with interest. If we assume that $300,000 of serial bonds were issued for construction of a fire station and that they are to be paid over a 10-year period beginning in 19X3, equal serial payments would require that $30,000 be repaid each year. If we further assume that the bonds pay interest at a rate of 7 percent annually, the amount necessary to pay principal and interest for the first year would be $51,000 [$30,000 principal and $21,000 interest ($300,000 × .07 = $21,000)]. In order for the governmental entity to pay this debt service, $51,000 would have to be appropriated as part of planned general fund transfers for the 19X3 fiscal year. Assuming that this transaction is recorded on July 15, 19X3, the entry in the general fund would be

```
Operating Transfer Out—Debt Service Fund ......... 51,000
    General Fund Cash ........................................ 51,000
```

The cash is transferred to the debt service fund which accounts for the receipt of money as follows:

```
Debt Service Fund Cash ............................... 51,000
    Operating Transfer In—General Fund .................... 51,000
```

The payment of the debt would be recorded in the debt service fund as:

```
Expenditure for General Obligation Bond Principal .. 30,000
Expenditure for General Obligation Bond Interest ... 21,000
    Debt Service Fund Cash .................................. 51,000
```

Also, the change in the status of long-term debt is recorded within the general long-term debt account group. The account group maintains a record of the principal owed and of the total amount to be provided to retire the principal. In order to reclassify the amount to be provided to the amount available, the following entry would be made at the time cash is transferred from the general fund to the debt service fund or at year-end:

```
Amount Available for Repayment of General Long-
    Term Debt ............................................ 30,000
    Amount to Be Provided for Repayment of
        General Long-Term Debt .............................. 30,000
```

Upon payment of the principal, the following entry would be made:

```
General Obligation Bonds Payable .................... 30,000
    Amount Available for Repayment of General
        Long-Term Debt ......................................... 30,000
```

Interest that accrues each year and is paid during the year is not recorded in the general long-term debt group. A summary of the interfund transactions associated with payment of principal and interest is provided in Exhibit 4-2, item 6.

Generally, long-term debt is used to acquire long-term assets. By the use of debt, public organization policy makers effectively shift the burden of paying for the services provided by long-term assets to future taxpayers who will both enjoy the benefits of services provided by the assets and who will be taxed to retire debt and interest incurred to provide them.

In addition to long-term debt obligations resulting from the issuance of bonds, obligations resulting from capital leases should be recorded in the long-term debt account group. For example, if the present value of a capital lease obligation is determined to be $30,000 at the inception of the lease, the following entry would be made in the account group:

Amount to Be Provided for Payment of Capital		
Lease Obligation......................................	30,000	
Capital Lease Obligation Payable..........................		30,000

Accounting for lease payments would follow the same procedure as that for bond payments except that payment normally is made from the general fund rather than the debt service fund.

SUMMARY

Governmental funds use a budgetary cycle to reflect the sequence of accounting events that occurs during a fiscal period. Budgetary accounts are established at the beginning of the fiscal year and are closed at the end of the fiscal year to provide current information about the degree to which operating results conform to budget expectations and to provide accounting controls on public organization managers. Collection of revenues, purchase of goods, payments to vendors, recording the budget, and closing the budget are all important events in the budgetary cycle. In addition to the budgetary cycle, governments use account groups to record fixed assets and long-term debt relating to the governmental funds. These account groups are established outside the governmental funds of the governmental unit to retain the budget-period focus of accounting and reporting in the governmental funds and to provide necessary planning information for oversight boards and managers.

The following key ideas and concepts were presented in this chapter:

1 Budgetary accounting is used by governmental funds, especially by the general fund, to record estimated revenues and appropriations (authorized expenditures). At the end of an accounting period, actual revenues are compared to estimated revenues through the closing process. Similarly, actual expenditures are compared to appropriations and encumbrances and are closed to fund balance(s).

2 Accounting transactions recorded in governmental funds are oriented primarily to reporting the results of operations, budget information, and resources that are available for current period expenditures. Long-term assets and liabilities are separated from the general fund and are reported in special accounting entities called account groups.

3 Transactions that involve general revenues and related expenditures for goods and services to be received and used in the current fiscal year are recorded primarily in the general fund. A special revenue fund is used for recording revenues that are restricted by some external authority to be used for a special purpose, for example, federal grants for highway construction.

4 Governments record encumbrances to prevent overexpenditure of appropriations by managers of governmental funds and to provide useful management information for oversight groups. Encumbrances reduce the balance in the appropriation account available for future purchase orders. When the goods or services are received, the encumbrances are reversed and replaced by actual expenditure amounts.

5 Transactions that involve acquiring or disposing of fixed assets or issuing or paying long-term debt frequently require transactions to be recorded simultaneously in several funds and account groups.

KEY CONCEPTS AND TERMS

Unreserved fund balance
Budgetary cycle
Budgetary accounts
Appropriations
Estimated revenues
Other financing sources
Other financing uses
Operating transfers out
Operating transfers in
Subsidiary account
Residual equity transfers
Quasi-external transaction
Control account
Tax levy

Self-assessed tax
Encumbrances
Reserve for encumbrances
Closing the accounts
Investment in general fixed assets
Amount to be provided for repayment of debt
Amount available for repayment of debt
Bonds payable
General obligation bonds
Revenue bonds
Serial debt

DISCUSSION QUESTIONS

1 List the steps in the budgetary cycle. Why is the budgetary cycle important for governmental units?

2 What are budgetary accounts? Why are they used by governmental units? Which funds are likely to use budgetary accounts?

3 What events may result in a change in the Unreserved Fund Balance account?

4 What are other financing sources and uses? Why are they separated from revenues and expenditures?

5 What are operating transfers? Why are they used by governmental funds?

6 Under what circumstances can the appropriations of a governmental unit be in excess of the estimated revenues of that unit?

7 How are subsidiary accounts used by governmental units in recording revenues and expenditures?

8 When are property taxes recorded? What amount is recorded? Why?

9 Why are many taxes other than property taxes not recorded by governmental units until cash is received?

10 What are residual equity transfers? How do they differ from interfund loans or operating transfers?

11 What is a quasi-external transaction? When would this transaction be recorded?

12 When are intergovernmental transfers recorded?
13 What is the purpose of the Encumbrances account? When are encumbrances recorded by governmental units? What account is credited when encumbrances are recorded?
14 What purposes do closing entries serve for governmental units? Which accounts are affected by closing entries?
15 What accounts are found in the general fixed asset account group? What do the amounts in these accounts represent?
16 What is the purpose of the Reserve for Inventory of Supplies account? When is it used?
17 What journal entries will be made in a governmental fund when a fixed asset is purchased? Where will these entries be made?
18 How is depreciation treated for governmental fund fixed assets? Why?
19 How is the disposal of governmental fund fixed assets recorded? Why?
20 Where are the long-term obligations of governmental funds recorded? Why?
21 What do the Amount to Be Provided and Amount Available for Payment of Long-Term Debt accounts represent? Under what circumstances are these accounts debited and credited?
22 What is the relationship between the debt service fund and the general long-term debt account group?
23 What is the relationship between fixed assets and long-term debt in governmental funds?

PROBLEMS

1 The budget for the City of Center Ridge contains the following estimated revenues and appropriations:

Estimated revenues:	
Property taxes	$3,000,000
Sales taxes	1,400,000
User fees	600,000
Bond proceeds	1,000,000
Appropriations:	
Public protection	750,000
Education	1,200,000
Streets and highways	860,000
Health and welfare	670,000
Parks and recreation	340,000
Administration	290,000
Water and sewage	500,000
Capital improvements	1,300,000

Required:
Provide the journal entry to record this information in the general fund journal for Center Ridge.

2 On June 1, 19X1, the City of Red Mountain levied property taxes in the amount of $2,500,000. All taxes are due by the end of the fiscal year. Historically, approximately 5 percent of the assessed taxes have been uncollectible. By July 1, 19X1, 60

percent of the taxes that were levied had been received. In addition, $4,600 of parking fees were collected during June. Fifty percent of the parking fees will be transferred to a special revenue fund for street improvements.

Required:
Record these events as they would appear in the Red Mountain's general fund journal.

3 As part of the appropriations for the Town of Blue Bayou, $300,000 was provided for travel expenses for the general government. The following data and transactions relate to the month of October, the first month of the Town's fiscal year: **(a)** The beginning balance in the account was $300,000. **(b)** $80,000 of airline tickets were ordered. **(c)** Part of the order, originally estimated at $60,000, was received. The actual invoice price for the portion received was $58,200. **(d)** Checks for $47,600 were written in partial payment of the invoices.

Required:
Set up a ledger account for travel expenditures as of October 1. Provide journal entries to record the transactions in Blue Bayou's general fund. Post these transactions to the ledger account as appropriate.

4 The budget for the City of Orange Bay's general fund contains the following estimated revenues and appropriations:

Estimated revenues:	
Property taxes	$6,000,000
Sales taxes	2,800,000
User fees	700,000
Appropriations:	
Public protection	1,750,000
Education	2,600,000
Streets and highways	1,340,000
Health and welfare	1,860,000
Parks and recreation	840,000
Administration	530,000

The actual revenues and expenditures for the general fund were as follows:

Revenues:	
Property taxes	$5,870,000
Sales taxes	2,910,000
User fees	745,000
Expenditures:	
Public protection	1,880,000
Education	2,560,000
Streets and highways	1,375,000
Health and welfare	1,840,000
Parks and recreation	810,000
Administration	550,000

Required:
Provide the closing entries necessary to record these events in Orange Bay's general fund journal.

5 In March 19X1, the County of Little Creek purchased a new police car with general fund revenues. The cost of the car was $16,000. In August 19X1, the car was involved in an accident that resulted in major uninsured damage to the vehicle. The car was sold as junk for $300.

Required:
Record these events in the journals of Little Creek's general fund and general fixed asset account group.

6 The following transactions relate to the Town of Twin Mills' general fund for 19X1:
  a Property taxes for $850,000 were billed. Four percent is assumed to be uncollectible.
  b A short-term note to a bank for $200,000 was issued.
  c The Town created an internal stores fund. A residual equity transfer of $50,000 was made by the general fund.
  d The general fund made a loan to the capital projects fund of $10,000.
  e Property taxes in the amount of $600,000 were received.
  f The loan to the bank plus $5,000 interest was repaid.
  g A grant was awarded to the Town by the state government. $25,000 of the grant is unrestricted. $75,000 is restricted for educational improvements. Under the terms of the restricted grant, actual costs will be reimbursed.
  h A payment of $10,000 is made by the general fund to a utility owned by the Town for payment of water and electricity.
  i The $25,000 unrestricted grant is received from the State.
  j Expenditures of $7,000 are made under the terms of the restricted grant. A bill is submitted to the state and a check is received for this amount.

Required:
Record each of the transactions in the general fund journal for the Town of Twin Mills.

7 The County of Cold Lake recorded $350,000 of encumbrances in 19X1. At fiscal year-end, $320,000 of these encumbrances had been cleared. The remaining balance was carried over to 19X2. The actual costs associated with these encumbrances paid during 19X2 amounted to $32,000.

Required:
Provide summary journal entries necessary to record all of the transactions for encumbrances in 19X1 and 19X2.

8 Purple Mountain had a balance of general fund supplies on hand at the beginning of 19X1 of $12,000. During 19X1, $94,000 of supplies were purchased for cash. Encumbrances were not used. The balance of supplies on hand at the end of 19X1 was $8,300.

Required:

Provide journal entries to record the transactions for 19X1 for the general fund.

9 On May 5, 19X1, the Village of Otter Springs issued $5,000,000 of 10-year general obligation serial bonds for building construction. The bonds sold at par to yield 8 percent interest. The proceeds were transferred to a capital projects fund for building construction. On March 1, 19X2, the Village's general fund transferred $900,000 to the debt service fund for payment of principal and interest due May 1. On May 1, 19X2, the principal and interest were paid.

Required:

Record these transactions as they would appear in Otter Springs' general, debt service, and capital project funds and in the general long-term debt account group.

5

Extending the Basic Accounting Cycle

Chapter 4 discussed the basic accounting and budgetary cycle for governmental units. This chapter extends the discussion to include certain transactions of governmental units that are more complex than those in the prior chapter. In addition, this chapter discusses briefly certain transactions of nonprofit organizations other than governmental units.

PROPERTY TAX ASSESSMENT AND COLLECTION

Property taxes generate a large portion of total revenues for most local governments. These taxes are known as **ad valorem** taxes because they are based on property value. A **property tax assessment** is an appraisal of the value of the property made for the purpose of determining its taxable value. Property taxes normally are based on a percentage of the assessed value. The legal action to bill taxpayers for property taxes is called a **tax levy** and is established by statute of the governing body. Property taxes are normally accounted for in the general fund and then are subsequently distributed to other funds as appropriate. However, taxes also may be levied for special purposes. Therefore, they may be accounted for in a special revenue capital projects or debt service fund created for such special-purpose levies.

Revenue Realization

The general rule regarding the realization of property taxes is that they are recorded as revenue of the current period if they are collectible during the current fiscal year or within a limited period of time after fiscal year-end. Traditionally, this period has been 60 days. An assumption of this rule is that taxes collected within 60 days after year-end effectively are available to pay for commitments made prior to year-end. Those taxes which have been levied but are not collectible within this period should be recorded as deferred revenue to be realized in the subsequent accounting period.

Accounting will change to the accrual basis from the current modified accrual basis in 1994. Property taxes will be recognized as revenue in the fiscal period for which taxes are levied if taxes are demanded by the end of the period, regardless of when cash is received. Taxes will be considered demanded if they are due before the end of the fiscal period. The amount recognized should be reduced by the amount estimated to be uncollectible.

The property tax collection cycle is described in Exhibit 5-1. The cycle begins at the top of the circle when the governmental unit levies taxes and bills taxpayers. It continues in a clockwise direction around the circle until all taxes are either collected or written off as uncollectible. In many situations, it is probable that the property tax collection cycle will not coincide with the fiscal year. Thus, the cycle will begin and end during different fiscal years. Further, each tax levy will have its own collection cycle (as illustrated); therefore, a governmental unit could be at different points in the cycle for different levies at any point in time. This situation, in which a governmental unit is involved in a number of levies with differing beginning dates and life cycles, is frequently

EXHIBIT 5-1
PROPERTY TAX COLLECTION CYCLE

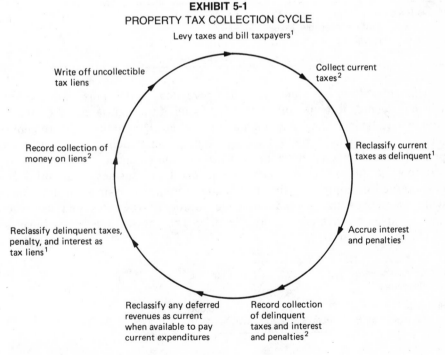

Levy taxes and bill taxpayers[1]

Write off uncollectible tax liens

Collect current taxes[2]

Record collection of money on liens[2]

Reclassify current taxes as delinquent[1]

Reclassify delinquent taxes, penalty, and interest as tax liens[1]

Accrue interest and penalties[1]

Reclassify any deferred revenues as current when available to pay current expenditures

Record collection of delinquent taxes and interest and penalties[2]

[1] Date to record established by statute.

[2] Record transaction as often as payments are received.

encountered in governmental accounting and will result in the recording of adjusting entries prior to the preparation of financial reports.

In addition to the realization issue described above, a governmental unit with material taxes receivable outstanding at year-end should provide for the possibility that some of the taxes which have been accrued may not be collected. In order to provide the managers of a governmental entity with proper information on which to base spending decisions, an allowance for uncollectible taxes should be established. Such allowances are based on the expectation of uncollectibility in the population of receivables on hand and are derived through an examination of past experience with the collection of such receivables. As is the case with business organization accounting, the estimate can be based on a percentage of taxes levied or can be developed by aging the receivables and providing a proper allowance for uncollectibles based on an estimate of collectibility.

As an example, assume a $1,500,000 property tax levy. Two percent of the levied property taxes are estimated to be uncollectible. Further, assume that 10 percent will not be collected within a short period after fiscal year-end. If we assume that the levy becomes binding on taxpayers as of June 1, an accountant would properly record such a levy at that date as follows:

Taxes Receivable—Current	1,500,000	
Allowance for Uncollectible Taxes—Current		30,000
Deferred Revenues		150,000
Revenues		1,320,000

This entry directly reduces recorded revenues for that portion of the levy which is deemed to be uncollectible. The focus of the transaction is on the resources available to the governmental unit, rather than on the measurement of income. In business organization accounting, an expense ("bad debt expense") would have been established with a debit balance.

Important differences between governmental and business accounting can be observed in comparing the transactions for the governmental unit above with the entries that would be made to record revenues and estimated uncollectibles by a business organization. The transactions for a business would be recorded as:

Accounts Receivable	1,500,000	
Revenues		1,500,000
Bad Debt Expense	30,000	
Allowance for Bad Debts		30,000

The total amount earned by the sale of goods or services is recorded as revenue by a business at the time the revenues are earned (goods are transferred or services are provided). Bad debt expense is estimated and recorded independently of the revenues since these expenses result from the credit policies of the business and are an expense of operations.

A governmental fund recognizes revenue in the current period only if the resulting resources are expendable for services provided during the current period. When taxes are uncollectible or collection will occur during a future period, the resources represented by the taxes are not available for current period services. Therefore, they are not revenues of the current period.

A summary entry reflecting assumed collection of the property taxes during the last seven months of 19X1 is as follows:

Cash... 1,200,000	
Taxes Receivable—Current............................ 1,200,000	

The difference between the Allowance for Uncollectible Taxes account and the Taxes Receivable—Current account is an estimate of the net realizable value of tax collections. The usual circumstance faced by a governmental unit is one in which not all property owners will pay their taxes. Since a government cannot rely on 100 percent of all taxes being collected and must focus its accounting process on resources available to the governmental unit, it cannot record revenues and authorize expenditures for the total amount of the tax levy. If an allowance account is not used, the governmental unit might appropriate more money than it expects to receive.

Current Classification of Receivables

Since the collectibility of taxes is a primary focus of financial reporting, it is customary to separate nondelinquent taxes receivable from those that have become delinquent. Therefore, at a legally established date, the taxes levied but not collected will become delinquent and should be recorded as such by reclassifying them as delinquent. The following entry is an example of such a transaction under the assumption that $300,000 remains in the Taxes Receivable—Current account on December 31, 19X1, and that the Allowance for Uncollectible Taxes balance of $30,000 relates entirely to the $300,000 of delinquent accounts:

Taxes Receivable—Delinquent..................... 300,000	
Allowance for Uncollectible Current Taxes........ 30,000	
Allowance for Uncollectible Delinquent Taxes.......... 30,000	
Taxes Receivable—Current............................. 300,000	

Once the taxes are declared legally delinquent, interest and penalties required by statute begin to accrue on these receivables. Under the assumption that the amount of interest and penalties receivable for the $300,000 in delinquent taxes is $12,000 on December 31, 19X1, the following entry would be appropriate:

Interest and Penalties Receivable...................... 12,000	
Revenues	12,000

Payment of delinquent taxes of $80,000 with related interest and penalties of $4,000 would be recorded as follows:

Cash.. 84,000	
Taxes Receivable—Delinquent............................	80,000
Interest and Penalties Receivable	4,000

In this example, we assumed that $150,000 of revenue was deferred when the tax levy was originally recorded. At some point during the tax collection cycle these deferred revenues will be reclassified as current revenues. The test which must be satisfied before the taxes are reclassified as realized is that they are or will be collectible in time to finance expenditures of the current fiscal year or within a reasonable period after fiscal year-end. Since this test was not satisfied originally, a deferral of revenue was recorded. When the realization of the deferred revenue is appropriate, it will be recorded as revenue. It is helpful to remember that the tax collection cycle is based on legally established due dates, not the fiscal year. The entry to reclassify deferred revenues as realized revenues would be:

Deferred Revenues.................................... 150,000	
Revenues	150,000

Liens—Subsequent Treatment of Receivables

If delinquent taxes are not paid, a lien will normally be issued against the property. A **tax lien** is a legal document which prevents sale or transfer of the property without payment of the amount for which the lien is issued. In effect, the governmental unit is able to force payment of the obligation by preventing its sale or transfer without release of the lien. The conversion of delinquent taxes into liens generally occurs on a date prescribed by law. The following entry would be appropriate at the date of such a lien:

Tax Liens Receivable... 228,000	
Allowance for Uncollectible Delinquent Taxes............. 30,000	
Allowance for Uncollectible Tax Liens..........................	30,000
Taxes Receivable—Delinquent...................................	220,000
Interest and Penalties Receivable..............................	8,000

Note that both the amount of delinquent taxes and the accrued interest and penalties become a tax lien. The Allowance for Uncollectible Interest and Pen-

Penalties account should be closed as well as all delinquent taxes and related interest and penalties which have been included in the tax lien.The final step in the tax collection cycle will be to record collection of amounts due on tax liens and to write off any uncollectible balance that will not be collected. Non-collectibility might occur even though the government has a lien against the property. For example, the property may be abandoned and/or in such disre-pair that the amount obtained from foreclosure and sale will still not discharge the amount due; hence an uncollectible tax lien results. In some cases, there may be no buyer for the property so the government is left with a tax lien on worthless property.

If we assume that $200,000 is received in cash on the lien receivables pre-viously established, the following entry is an example of how the final collec-tion on tax liens would be recorded:

Cash	200,000	
Allowance for Uncollectible Tax Liens	28,000	
Tax Liens Receivable		228,000

Last, the Allowance for Uncollectible Tax Liens account must be closed since all liens are assumed to have been collected or written off against the allowance account:

Allowance for Uncollectible Tax Liens	2,000	
Revenues		2,000

Exhibit 5-2 reviews the account balances and examines the impact of what has been recorded as a result of assumed circumstances.

These transactions complete the tax collection cycle. All accounts are now closed except for Cash and Revenues both of which have balances of $1,484,000. The original levy was $1,500,000 of which $28,000 was determined to be uncollectible. Twelve thousand dollars of interest and penalties were col-lected which produced a net cash inflow of $1,484,000. The Revenues account will be closed together with other budgetary accounts when the fiscal year ends. As noted earlier, the tax collection cycle does *not* generally coincide with the fiscal year, so final write-off of delinquent taxes representing the com-pletion of the tax collection cycle may occur at a different time than fiscal year-end.

CAPITAL PROJECTS

Expenditures for assets that are to be constructed are more complex than other purchase transactions since the funds may be expended over multiple fiscal periods. In such circumstances, construction costs should be recorded in a capital projects fund. Long-term debt frequently is used to pay for capital

EXHIBIT 5-2
ACCOUNT BALANCES FROM PROPERTY TAX CYCLE

Account	Debits	Credits	Balance
Taxes Receivable—Current	$1,500,000	$1,200,000	$
		300,000	0
Allowance for Uncollectible Taxes—Current	30,000	30,000	0
Taxes Receivable—Delinquent	300,000	80,000	
		220,000	0
Allowance for Uncollectible Taxes—			
Delinquent	30,000	30,000	0
Interest and Penalties Receivable	12,000	4,000	
		8,000	0
Allowance for Uncollectible Tax Liens	28,000		
	2,000	30,000	0
Tax Liens Receivable	228,000	228,000	0
Cash	1,200,000		
	84,000		
	200,000		1,484,000
Revenues		1,320,000	
		12,000	
		150,000	
		2,000	1,484,000
Deferred Revenues	150,000	150,000	0

projects and also must be recorded. A typical capital project cycle for the construction of a building is described in Exhibit 5-3. The capital projects cycle begins at the top of the circle when the project is authorized by the governing body and continues until the building is complete and the fund is closed. The capital project cycle continues around the circle during the life of the project (which may extend across several fiscal years until the building is completed).

As an example of how a governmental unit might record a capital project, assume that the residents of the City of East River wish to finance construction of a fire station. Authorization for the construction and for issuance of long-term bonds to pay for the project must come from the City Council. In some cases, local residents would vote on whether or not the bonds could be issued. Once legal approval is received and an estimate of the cost of the project is secured, an appropriation would be made. If we assume that the appropriation was for $400,000 on October 1, 19X1, 75 percent of which is to be paid from bonds and 25 percent is to be paid from a federal grant, the transaction would be recorded in a capital projects fund as follows:

Estimated Funds for Construction 400,000
    Appropriation... 400,000

EXHIBIT 5-3
CAPITAL PROJECTS FUND CYCLE

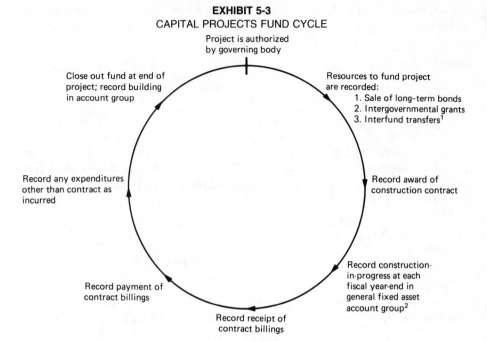

¹ These are the most common sources of revenues to fund capital projects;
any combination of these may occur or other sources are possible.

² The capital project cycle does not coincide with the entity's fiscal year.

A "memo" entry could be used instead of this journal entry to note the authorization to spend resources:

Construction approved for $400,000 by City Council on October 1, 19X1.

Under the assumption that the bonds are issued at face value and that the federal grant is awarded but not received, cash and receivables would be recorded in the capital projects fund as follows:

Cash.. 300,000
Due from Federal Government 100,000
    Other Financing Sources—Bond Proceeds............ 300,000
    Revenues 100,000

This transaction would result in an obligation and expenditure on the books of the federal government in the amount of $100,000.

Expenditures and encumbrances are recorded in the capital projects fund in the same manner as in the general fund. For example, the award of a $400,000 construction contract for the construction of the fire station would be recorded as follows:

```
Encumbrances....................................... 400,000
    Reserve for Encumbrances............................. 400,000
```

The contract is recorded in the same manner as a purchase order would have been recorded.

An interim billing for $100,000 received from the contractor for work completed to date would be recorded as follows, assuming that the contract provided that 10 percent would be retained until the project is satisfactorily completed and inspected:

```
Reserve for Encumbrances ...................... 100,000
Expenditures ...................................... 100,000
    Encumbrances........................................... 100,000
    Contracts Payable....................................... 90,000
    Contracts Payable—Retained Percentage............. 10,000
```

Payment of the $90,000 due to the contractor would be recorded as follows:

```
Contracts Payable................................ 90,000
    Cash ................................................... 90,000
```

When money is received from the federal grant, the following entry is made:

```
Cash............................................... 100,000
    Due from Federal Government......................... 100,000
```

Assume that the city's fiscal year-end occurs at this stage of the project. It is necessary to reflect the value of construction completed to date in the general fixed assets account group:

```
Construction-in-Progress—Fire Station.......... 100,000
    Investment in General Fixed Assets—
        Federal Grant/Long-Term Bonds......... 100,000
```

When expenditures are made on construction in progress, the general fixed asset account group must reflect the value of the asset constructed to date. Exhibit 5-4, item 1, summarizes these interfund and account group transactions.

The closing entries at fiscal year-end will close all budgetary accounts in the capital projects fund as follows:

EXHIBIT 5-4
SUMMARY OF INTERFUND AND ACCOUNT GROUP TRANSACTIONS
[ALL NUMBERS IN $000, CREDITS IN ( )]

Account title	General fund	Capital projects fund	General fixed asset group
1. Asset construction:			
Expenditures		$100	
Contracts Payable		(90)	
Contracts Payable—Retained Percentage		(10)	
Contracts Payable		90	
Cash		(90)	
Construction-in-Progress			$100
Investment in General Fixed Assets			(100)
2. Completion of Construction:			
Expenditure—Prior Year		300	
Contracts Payable		(270)	
Contracts Payable—Retained Percentage		(30)	
Contracts Payable—Retained Percentage		40	
Contracts Payable		270	
Cash		(310)	
Buildings			400
Construction-in-Progress			(100)
Investment in General Fixed Assets			(300)

Appropriations..................................... 400,000	
Encumbrances...	300,000
Expenditures...	100,000
Revenues... 100,000	
Other Financing Sources—Bond Proceeds..... 300,000	
Estimated Funds for Construction	400,000

Exhibit 5-5 summarizes the account balances for the capital projects fund after all entries for the fiscal year have been recorded in the accounts. The only accounts remaining are Cash, Reserve for Encumbrances, and Contracts Payable—Retained Percentage.

If the fire station is completed in the next fiscal year and the contractor submits a final billing of $300,000, the entry would be:

Expenditures—Prior Year 300,000	
Contracts Payable......................................	270,000
Contracts Payable—Retained Percentage.............	30,000

The Expenditures—Prior Year account is used since the appropriations for these expenditures were made last year. No additional appropriations were made for the current year.

EXHIBIT 5-5

CAPITAL PROJECTS FUND ACCOUNT BALANCES

Account title	Debits	Credits	Balance
Estimated Funds for Construction	$400,000	$400,000	$0
Appropriations	400,000	400,000	0
Cash	300,000	90,000	
	100,000		310,000
Due from Federal Government	100,000	100,000	0
Other Financing Sources	300,000	300,000	0
Revenues	100,000	100,000	0
Encumbrances	400,000	100,000	
		300,000	0
Reserve for Encumbrances	100,000	400,000	(300,000)
Expenditures	100,000	100,000	0
Contracts Payable	90,000	90,000	0
Contracts Payable—Retained Percentage		10,000	(10,000)

The building is then normally inspected and certified as satisfactorily completed prior to the time that the final bill is paid. Under the assumption that the contractor's work has been satisfactory, the following entry would record the completion of the project:

Contracts Payable—Retained Percentage	40,000	
Contracts Payable	270,000	
Cash		310,000

The only remaining entry necessary to close out all accounts in the capital projects fund would be to close the Expenditures—Prior Year and Reserve for Encumbrances:

Reserve for Encumbrances..........................	300,000	
Expenditures—Prior Year................................		300,000

If any money had remained unexpended, it normally would be transferred to the general fund or debt service fund in order to close the capital projects fund at the end of the project. It is important to remember that the life cycle of a project often crosses fiscal years and that the life of the fund is defined by the length of time required to complete the project.

In order to record the new fire station in the general fixed assets account group, an additional related entry will be required:

Buildings—Fire Station................................	400,000	
Construction-in-Progress—Fire Station		100,000
Investment in General Fixed Assets—		
Federal Grant/Long-Term Bonds......................		300,000

The expenditures recorded in the capital projects fund eventually appear as the total debit to the asset account in the general fixed assets account group.

A summary of these interfund and account group transactions is provided in Exhibit 5-4, item 2.

SPECIAL ASSESSMENTS

Special assessments result from a tax levy against property owners on a selected base such as feet of frontage or assessed valuation of property in order to finance a particular activity. Although these taxes are considered an assessment, they are similar to a user fee in that affected property owners who benefit from the activity provide the revenue. A common example of a special assessment is to pay for curbs and gutters. Each property owner is assessed per lineal foot of frontage for the new curbs and gutters capital improvement project. The government in turn borrows funds to finance the construction of the new curbs and gutters and permits property owners to repay the government at the same rate that the bondholders are repayed. This type of project is presumed to benefit property holders and the citizenry by providing a common standard for the capital improvement (all curbs and gutters look alike, for example) and permit property holders to borrow the money through the government's tax-exempt status at a lower rate than they would have to borrow to finance the project privately.

The capital improvement assessment which benefits specific property owners is accounted for and reported in the capital projects fund and the debt service fund. The long-term debt issued is reported in the general long-term debt account group if the government is liable for repayment, either directly (because the bonds represent a general obligation full faith and credit pledge of the government) or indirectly (as a secondary source of funds for repayment if the property owners fail to make sufficient payment to service the debt).

Another type of special assessment project is a service-type assessment. In this case, citizens of the government choose to pay a special property tax assessment for services such as snow plowing, libraries, pollution control, or other services which would normally be paid by a general or special revenue fund. These service-type assessments should be accounted for in the general or special revenue fund, as appropriate, or may be reported in an enterprise fund. The fund type should be selected which best reflects the service-type activity being financed. Any debt associated with this service-type assessment which has a governmental pledge (full faith and credit, general obligation, or otherwise) must be disclosed in the general long-term debt account group as "Special Assessment Debt with Governmental Commitment."

Prior to a recent GASB regulation, special assessments were reported in a separate fund type, special assessment funds. However, reporting for this fund frequently created an "artificial deficit" when expenditures were made for projects before revenues were received from property owners. This deficit, which was disclosed in the general-purpose financial statements, was perceived to unfavorably bias or mislead users of financial statements. Therefore, the special assessments fund type was eliminated for external financial reporting although it may still be used for internal purposes.

PROPRIETARY FUNDS

Proprietary funds are used to account for segments of a governmental unit that are intended to operate in a manner similar to a business organization. The concepts of capital maintenance and return on invested capital normally govern the management and accounting policies of such governmental entities. Proprietary funds may exist primarily to provide services to citizens external to the government (enterprise funds) or they may exist primarily to provide services to other departments within the government (internal service funds).

Enterprise Funds

Proprietary funds often represent "businesses" run by a governmental entity. Such governmental businesses are created because it may be in the public interest for governments to provide services that may be sold to its customers, particularly if these businesses can operate most efficiently as monopolies. Service areas in which governments may choose to operate enterprise funds might include health, parking, utilities, and public transportation. Because of the large investment in capital facilities necessary to provide these services, sometimes it is not cost effective to maintain more than one organization to provide the services in a particular geographic area. In this situation, the service provider has a monopoly on the service. Therefore, costs and prices are not controlled by a competitive market. Accordingly, these organizations are nearly always either government owned or regulated.

If most of the cost of these services is borne by the user, and if public policy indicates that the most effective way to provide such services is through the sponsorship of a governmental unit, enterprise funds can be used to establish a fiscal entity to capture and report the transactions of these organizations. These entities operate like businesses except that their financial objectives may not be to maximize return on investment for their owners. Since the owners are the citizens of the government, the objective of the entity is usually to provide the service at a cost that will permit the entity to break even or earn a small return in excess of incurred cost.

However such an entity chooses to define its financial goals, it is usually true that the capital maintenance concept applies to accounting for these activities. Therefore, the entity is generally responsible for maintaining its capital investment, replacing its own fixed assets, and paying for its own debt service. Thus, in order to maintain accounting information for monitoring these requirements, transactions of these entities should be recorded in a proprietary fund rather than in the governmental funds and account groups.

Internal Service Funds

Some government business activities may exist primarily to serve the needs of the governmental unit. That is, the customers may be other departments of the government. Garages, motor pools, computer processing facilities, and supply centers may be created by a governmental unit to serve the needs of its other departments. The costs of these internal services are covered by charges to other departments just as though the internal service departments were operating as businesses. Thus, internal service funds follow the same accounting procedures as enterprise (external service) funds.

Example Transactions

The normal transactions of proprietary funds are described below and are similar to those which would be recorded for a business. The concept underlying the accounting for these transactions is based on (business organization) accrual accounting that normally is used in these funds.

Revenues Enterprise or internal service funds recognize the revenue from the sale of services to customers on an accrual basis. That is, the earning process associated with such services must be essentially complete, receivables associated with recording revenue must be reasonably measurable and collectible, and there can be no important and material costs which are uncertain.

For example, assume that an electric utility sells $200,000 of power to the general fund and sells $1,300,000 of power to customers other than the governmental unit. Further, assume that the accountant for the enterprise fund estimates that the enterprise fund will experience $50,000 in expense through uncollectible accounts associated with these revenues. In such circumstances, the following entries would be appropriate:

Due from General Fund	200,000	
Accounts Receivable	1,300,000	
Operating Revenues		1,500,000
Uncollectible Accounts Expense	50,000	
Allowance for Uncollectible Accounts		50,000

The enterprise fund may receive an intergovernmental grant for a specific purpose, such as pollution control, which would be recorded as **Nonoperating Revenues.** This account is similar to Other Financing Sources for governmental funds in that it is intended to distinguish nonoperating activity from regular operating activity in the financial statements. Under the assumption that the enterprise fund was the recipient of a $1,000,000 grant from the federal government, the following entry would be appropriate:

Due from Federal Government	1,000,000	
Nonoperating Revenues		1,000,000

The collection of $1,240,000 from customers, $200,000 from the general fund, and $1,000,000 from the federal government is recorded as follows:

Cash	2,440,000
Accounts Receivable	1,240,000
Due from General Fund	200,000
Due from Federal Government	1,000,000

Operating Expenses Enterprise funds will record the expenses associated with operations based on the matching principle. The following entry is provided under the assumption that bills for previously unrecorded operating expenses are received which relate to currently realized revenue:

Operating Expenses	780,000
Cash	780,000

Revenue Bonds The enterprise fund may issue revenue bonds to pay for capital expenditures. Revenue bonds are obligations which pledge revenues from a specific enterprise for repayment of the bond. For example, a city-owned utility which issues revenue bonds may pledge revenues from fees paid by customers for repayment of bond principal and payment of interest. Proprietary funds account for their own fixed assets (including depreciation) and long-term liabilities. Therefore, if an enterprise fund wants to purchase machinery to be used to produce its product or service, revenue bonds might be issued. Unlike general obligation bonds which are repaid from general revenues, revenue bond principal and interest is paid from the earnings of the proprietary fund.

For example, assume a public utility purchases new equipment for $5,000,000 through issuance of $4,000,000 in revenue bonds and from the federal grant previously recorded. The appropriate entries would be:

Cash	4,000,000
Revenue Bonds Payable	4,000,000
Equipment	5,000,000
Cash	5,000,000

When interest accrues on the revenue bonds, it is recognized by the enterprise fund. Payment is made for interest and principal by the enterprise fund when they become due. If the revenue bonds issued above have $400,000 due in principal ($200,000) and interest ($200,000), the following entries would record this payment and related expense:

Nonoperating Expense—Interest	200,000	
Interest Payable		200,000
Interest Payable	200,000	
Revenue Bonds Payable	200,000	
Cash		400,000

Depreciation is recorded on long-term assets owned by proprietary funds consistent with a capital maintenance concept of accounting measurement. Under the assumption that $500,000 in depreciation expense is considered properly matched with the current period revenue, the depreciation on equipment would be recorded as follows:

Operating Expense—Depreciation	500,000	
Accumulated Depreciation—Equipment		500,000

Closing Entries The revenue and expense accounts must be closed at fiscal year-end to arrive at net income (loss) which increases (decreases) retained earnings. Based on the entries illustrated above, the following closing entries would be appropriate:

Operating Revenues	1,500,000	
Operating Expenses		780,000
Operating Expense—Depreciation		500,000
Doubtful Account Expense		50,000
Unreserved Retained Earnings		170,000
Nonoperating Revenues	1,000,000	
Nonoperating Expense—Interest		200,000
Unreserved Retained Earnings		800,000

Exhibit 5-6 summarizes the balances of the transactions recorded in the enterprise fund. The enterprise fund's balance sheet is provided in Exhibit 5-7.

FIDUCIARY FUNDS

Fiduciary funds are created to maintain records of transactions that involve resources that are not under the complete control of the governmental unit and may not be available for the provision of services by the government. Fiduciary funds include trust and agency funds.

EXHIBIT 5-6
ENTERPRISE FUND ACCOUNT BALANCES

Account title	Debits	Credits	Balance
Due from General Fund	$ 200,000	$ 200,000	$ 0
Accounts Receivable	1,300,000	1,240,000	60,000
Doubtful Accounts Expense		50,000	(50,000)
Operating Revenues	1,500,000	1,500,000	0
Cash	2,440,000	780,000	
	4,000,000	5,000,000	
		400,000	260,000
Due from Federal Government	1,000,000	1,000,000	0
Nonoperating Revenues	1,000,000	1,000,000	0
Operating Expenses	780,000	780,000	0
Depreciation Expense	500,000	500,000	0
Interest Payable	200,000	200,000	0
Interest Expense	200,000	200,000	0
Revenue Bonds Payable	200,000	4,000,000	(3,800,000)
Equipment	5,000,000		5,000,000
Accumulated Depreciation		500,000	(500,000)
Unreserved Retained Earnings		170,000	
		800,000	(970,000)

EXHIBIT 5-7
ENTERPRISE FUND BALANCE SHEET

Assets

Cash...		$ 260,000
Accounts receivable..	$ 60,000	
Allowance for uncollectible accounts..	50,000	10,000
Equipment..	$5,000,000	
Accumulated depreciation...	500,000	4,500,000
Total assets		$4,770,000

Liabilities and Retained Earnings

Revenue bonds payable..	$3,800,000
Unreserved retained earnings	970,000
Total liabilities and retained earnings.....................................	$4,770,000

Trust Funds

Trust funds are established for resources that are externally restricted, that is, over which the government does not have full discretionary control. For example, the government may agree to provide retirement benefits to its employees under a participatory plan. Under such an arrangement the government will make periodic pension contributions that are placed in a trust, usually with a third-party funding agent. The resources in the pension trust fund are invested and can be used only to pay retirement benefits to employees according to the retirement contract. Thus, the government is legally obligated to make the contributions and payments and does not have control over the use of the financial resources.

Trust funds sometimes result from donations to the government that carry restrictions imposed by the donor. For example, a donation of property may be made to establish a library or museum. Also, monetary resources, cash, or securities may be donated for a purpose designated by the donor. The donor may specify how the property or investments may be used and whether any part of the amount can be spent for operations. **Expendable trust** funds permit the expenditure of some portion of the original donation and the principal of the donation. **Nonexpendable trusts** permit only the expenditure of income from investment of the principal. Thus, one of the primary purposes of trust fund accounting is clear separation of the principal from income earned on the principal.

In nonexpendable trusts, the principal must be maintained intact and accrual accounting should be used. Accrual accounting separates assets from expenses and records depreciation on the assets in order to maintain the capital of the entity. Like a business, accounting for a nonexpendable trust is intended to ensure that operating resource transfers are made from the earnings of the entity rather than from the contributed capital. Frequently, the earnings from the principal of nonexpendable trust funds are transferred to another fund (for example, an expendable trust fund or special revenue fund) where the resources are used.

Since expendable trust funds permit the expenditure of the principal, the modified accrual basis of accounting is used. However, the resources and operation of the fund must be separated from those of the general government. Therefore, fund assets, including fixed assets and fund liabilities (short-term and long-term) are recorded in the trust fund accounts rather than in the governmental fund or group accounts.

Agency Funds

Agency funds record resources that are collected for other organizations (for example, other levels of government) with the anticipation that the resources will be further transferred in a short period of time. Therefore, there is normally no investment of these funds. For example, agency funds are established for payroll taxes that will be transferred to the state and federal governments. County governments frequently collect property taxes that may be shared by several units of government such as cities and special districts.

These funds record assets as the resources are collected that are offset by liabilities to the other units of government. When the resources are transferred, the appropriate entry is recorded to reflect the disbursement and retirement of the obligation. The modified accrual basis is used for such agency funds, although generally no revenues or expenditures are needed. Agency funds often do not appear in year-end financial statements since they should have no fund balance.

Agency funds should be viewed as accounting entities which operate as "pass-through" vehicles which enable financial accountability in agency situations and in which assets equal liabilities. Normally, such funds exist in circumstances in which one governmental unit acts as the agent for another. A common example would be the situation in which one governmental unit collects taxes for others and accounts for the tax levy and subsequent collection and transmittal in an agency fund. For example, the entry to record the levy of $200,000 in taxes by Forrest County for the City of East River (10 percent), the East River School District (40 percent), and the County's general fund (50 percent) would be:

Taxes Receivable 200,000		
Due to City of East River................................	20,000	
Due to East River Schools.............................	80,000	
Due to General Fund	100,000	

Under the assumption that the taxes are collected and distributed, the following entries would be appropriate:

Cash... 200,000		
Taxes Receivable	200,000	
Due to City of East River..........................	20,000	
Due to East River Schools	80,000	
Due to General Fund	100,000	
Cash	200,000	

Once these entries have been made, all account balances for the agency fund are zero.

The tax collection transactions reviewed earlier in the chapter which include entries for allowance accounts for uncollectible taxes and delinquencies would be maintained on the individual governmental unit books and in the County general fund rather than in the agency fund of the collecting agency.

COMPARISON OF GOVERNMENTAL AND OTHER NONPROFIT ORGANIZATIONS

Nonprofit organizations other than governments generally are grouped into four classes: colleges and universities, hospitals, voluntary health and welfare organizations, and (certain) other nonprofit organizations. The fourth class includes all nonprofit institutions that do not fit into one of the other classifications. These include cemetery organizations, civic organizations, fraternal organizations, labor unions, libraries, museums, cultural institutions, performing arts organizations, political parties, private and community organizations, private elementary and secondary schools, professional associations, public broadcasting stations, religious organizations, research and scientific organizations, social and country clubs, trade associations, zoological and botanical societies, among others.

Accounting for each of the four classes of nonprofit organizations is unique in certain respects; yet, in some ways it is similar to governmental accounting. Fund accounting is utilized by all types of nonprofit organizations, although the fund titles and basis of accounting used may differ. The same kinds of transactions often are observed across different classes of nonprofit organizations. The type of funds used in the four classes of nonprofit organizations are similar to funds used in governmental entities and are summarized in Exhibit 2-1 in Chapter 2.

Governmental entities currently use the modified accrual basis of accounting. Beginning in 1994, they will be required to use the accrual accounting basis as applied to a financial resources measurement focus as discussed in Chapter 1. Universities, hospitals, voluntary health and welfare, and other nonprofit organizations all use accrual accounting. However, the accrual process is applied differently within some of these organizations. For example, depreciation is recorded as an operating expense of hospitals, but traditionally has not been recorded by universities.

General operating activity is accounted for in the general fund for governments and in the current unrestricted fund for nonprofit organizations. Sometimes a hospital will use the title general fund instead of current unrestricted fund. Restricted funds received for current operating purposes generally are accounted for in the special revenue fund for governmental units, in the current restricted fund for universities, voluntary health and welfare, and other nonprofits, and in the restricted–specific-purpose fund for hospitals. Unrestricted resources which are appropriated or designated by the hospital's governing board are accounted for as part of the current unrestricted fund. In general, balance sheets should show a clear distinction between externally restricted resources and internally restricted resources for all four classes of nonprofit organizations.

The Financial Accounting Standards Board has proposed a new financial statement, statement of changes in net assets, for the four classes of nonprofit organizations. The statement is intended to describe the distinction between resources that are permanently restricted, those temporarily restricted, and those unrestricted.

Endowment funds in all four classes of nonprofit organizations account for donations for which the principal must remain intact. Investment income is transferred from the endowment fund to either the current unrestricted or restricted fund depending on the donor's specifications. If the donor does not specify the use, the investment income may be used for general operating activity. Annuity and life income funds are characteristic of universities but may appear in other nonprofit organizations. Annuity and life income funds account for donations of principal that will revert to the institution at the end of the annuity term or death of the donor in the case of life income donations. In annuity and life income funds the institution agrees to pay the donor a stipulated amount for a fixed term (annuity) or for the donor's life (life income). Gains and losses on sale of investments are accounted for within the annuity or life income fund.

Governmental entities generally do not have endowment funds. Instead, they use expendable trust (principal and income may be expended) or nonexpendable trust (income may be expended, principal may not be expended) funds to account for contributed resources.

Governmental entities account for fixed assets (without recording depreciation) in the general fixed assets account group and long-term debt with a full faith and credit pledge in the general long-term debt account group. The four classes of nonprofit organizations account for fixed assets and debt within funds and do not have any parallel to the account groups used by governmental entities. *FASB Statement 93* (effective for fiscal years beginning after May 15, 1988) requires nonprofit organizations that are not under the jurisdiction of governmental units to recognize depreciation in their external financial statements on all assets except certain works of art and historical treasures. *GASB Statement 8* (effective January 1988) requires that nonprofit organizations under government jurisdiction not record depreciation. The primary group of nonprofit organizations affected by the FASB/GASB dispute are government-supported colleges and universities. Government-supported colleges and universities do not record depreciation as an expense that is reflected in their financial operating statements, but a depreciation allowance and a provision for depreciation may be reported in the balance sheet of the plant funds. Hospitals, voluntary health and welfare organizations, and other nonprofit organizations already record depreciation in accordance with their respective AICPA Audit Guides; so they are not affected.

The four classes of nonprofit organizations record fixed assets and related liabilities within funds, but each class uses different funds for that purpose. Universities use a plant fund with four categories. The categories include unexpended (assets restricted for fixed asset purchases and related liabilities), plant renewal and replacement (assets available for capital maintenance or building projects), retirement of indebtedness (debt service funds), and investment in plant (assets, construction-in-progress, and related liabilities which finance the assets' construction). Hospitals account for property, plant, and equipment and related liabilities within the current unrestricted fund. Voluntary health and welfare organizations use a land, building, and equipment fund (sometimes referred to as a plant fund). The land, building, and equipment fund accounts for fixed assets, unexpended resources designated for purchase of fixed assets, gains or losses on sale of fixed assets, and liabilities incurred in the purchase of fixed assets recorded in the fund. Other nonprofits may record fixed assets and related liabilities in the current unrestricted fund or a plant fund.

Universities use loan funds to account for loans to faculty, students, and staff. Loan funds may be used by the other classes of nonprofit organizations but are not common in practice. Agency funds may be used by any nonprofit organization that acts as an agent for another organization in handling funds. An example of a purpose for an agency fund would be to collect and transfer employee contributions to an external retirement system.

The AICPA has issued a separate audit guide for each of the categories of nonprofit organizations. The FASB has proposed a financial reporting model for nonprofit organizations that would supersede the current AICPA audit guides and would provide a common format and content for the financial statements of hospitals, colleges and universities, voluntary health and welfare organizations, and other nonprofit organizations. In addition, colleges and universities have their own accounting manual issued by the National Association of College and University Business Officers. Hospitals also have active organizations that recommend accounting practices.[1]

Unique accounting practices exist in each of the four classes of nonprofit organizations. An overview of some of the more important of these differences is provided in the remainder of this section. For those who have a need for more in-depth discussion of these issues, reference should be made to the literature cited in footnote 1.

Public Schools

Public schools normally are not considered as a separate type of nonprofit organization since they generally are parts of governmental units or are separate governmental units. Accordingly, accounting for public schools is similar to accounting for other governmental units. The fund structure of public schools parallels that of governmental units, and similar types of transactions may be observed.[2]

Colleges and Universities

The funds used in college and university accounting include current unrestricted and current restricted funds, loan funds, endowment funds, annuity and life income funds, plant funds, and agency funds. Most major operating activities, such as tuition and fees, faculty and staff salaries, and general instructional support expenditures, are accounted for in the current unrestricted fund. Revenues and expenditures should only be recognized in the current un-

---

[1]Major industry publications include:
Audits of Colleges and Universities, 2d ed. (AICPA, 1975).
Audits of Voluntary Health and Welfare Organizations, 2d ed. (AICPA, 1988).
Hospital Audit Guide, 6th ed. (AICPA, 1985)
Audits of Certain Nonprofit Organizations, 2d ed. (AICPA, 1987).
College and University Business Administration: Administrative Service, National Association of College and University Business Officers, in Looseleaf Form with periodic Changes and Supplements (Washington, D.C.).

[2]*Financial Accounting for Local and State School Systems* and *Principles of Public School Accounting,* National Center for Education Statistics, 1980 and 1981.

restricted and current restricted funds of colleges and universities. Investment income from endowment, and from annuity or life income funds are transferred to the current restricted or unrestricted fund for expenditure depending upon the donor's restriction. Revenues and expenditures should be recognized on the accrual basis to the extent possible. Endowment, annuity, and life income funds record *additions* and *deductions,* not revenues and expenditures, since the inflows of resources in these funds are transferred to the current funds for use. Additions and deductions are reported in a statement of changes in fund balances.

Interfund transfers are classified as *mandatory* and *nonmandatory* depending on whether the transfer is made to comply with an externally imposed agreement such as a grant restriction or bond indenture.

Typical transactions of the current unrestricted fund would include

1 Recognition of amounts due for tuition and fees:

```
Accounts Receivable..............................3,000,000
    Allowance for Doubtful Accounts.......................  22,000
    Revenues ................................................2,978,000
```

If a term or semester bridges two fiscal years, the revenues and expenditures should be recognized in the fiscal year that the majority of the instruction takes place. Any amounts that are not recognized as applying this criteria should be recorded as deferred revenue.

Auxiliary enterprises include residence halls, food service, intercollegiate athletics, bookstores, etc., and should be accounted for within the current unrestricted fund.

2 Receipt of cash for tuition and fees:

```
Cash...................................................2,980,000
    Accounts Receivable ....................................2,980,000
```

3 Expenditures for educational purposes:

```
Expenditures .......................................1,650,000
    Accounts Payable........................................1,650,000
```

4 Transfers to other funds:

```
Mandatory Transfers.............................. 460,000
Nonmandatory Transfers.......................... 270,000
    Due to Plant Funds......................................... 730,000
```

Current restricted funds operate uniquely in that receipts are recorded as credits to the fund balance until expenditures take place and then an exactly equal amount of revenue is recognized. In other words, the revenue recognition criteria is that the expenditure must be incurred for the restricted purpose before the revenue can be accrued. Therefore, revenues always equal expenditures. This accounting is similar to the governmental revenue recognition criteria for restricted grants in which revenues are not recognized until the expenditure is made for the restricted grant purpose.

The entry to record a $9,000 restricted grant with $5,000 authorized for expenditure now and $4,000 later would be reflected as follows in the current restricted fund:

```
Cash.....................................................  9,000
      Fund Balance...............................................  4,000
      Revenues ...................................................  5,000

Expenditures ..........................................  5,000
      Cash .......................................................  5,000
```

Revenues are recognized only in an equal amount to expenditures authorized and expended in the current restricted fund. Subsequent expenditure of the $4,000 would be recorded as follows:

```
Fund Balance ..........................................  4,000
      Revenues ...................................................  4,000

Expenditures ..........................................  4,000
      Cash .......................................................  4,000
```

Since the revenues and expenditures of current restricted funds are offsetting (equal), the revenues are closed against the expenditures at year-end to zero out the fund.

There are three categories of endowment funds: endowment, term endowment, and quasi-endowment. Endowment funds account for the principal of the endowment to be retained intact within that fund and any investment earnings on the endowment must be transferred to the current restricted or unrestricted fund to be expended for the specified purpose. Term endowment funds permit expenditure of the principal upon passage of a specified time period or a particular event. Quasi-endowment funds are internally designated within the institution so the governing board may expend the principal at any time.

The accounting is the same for all three categories of endowment funds. For example, receipt of a $100,000 cash gift for endowment that specifies the earnings be used for scholarships would be recorded in the endowment fund as

```
Cash ...................................................  100,000
      Fund Balance ...............................................  100,000
```

The cash would then be invested in order to earn a return to be used for the purpose specified by the endowment:

```
Investments ........................................... 100,000
    Cash ........................................................ 100,000
```

Earnings of $10,000 on the endowment would be recognized in the Endowment Fund as:

```
Cash ...................................................... 10,000
    Investment Income—Restricted ........................... 10,000
```

Transfer of $10,000 endowment income to the current restricted fund would be recorded in the endowment fund as:

```
Endowment Income Appropriated ..................... 10,000
    Cash ...................................................... 10,000
```

This transaction would be recorded in the current restricted fund as:

```
Cash ...................................................... 10,000
    Endowment Income Appropriated ......................... 10,000
```

Expenditure of $10,000 of endowment income for scholarships in the current restricted fund would be recorded as:

```
Expenditure ............................................. 10,000
    Cash ...................................................... 10,000
```

In summary, no revenues or expenditures are recorded within the endowment fund itself; the income must be transferred to the current restricted fund for expenditure. The expenditure can be made only for the purpose for which the endowment was donated. Thus, the income and expenditure are recorded in a current restricted fund if a specific purpose is specified by the donor. If the purpose of the endowment is unrestricted or unspecified by the donor, the income would be transferred to the current unrestricted fund.

Plant funds account for resources restricted for plant investment or invested in fixed assets. *Unexpended plant funds* account for resources to be used for the purchase or construction of property, plant and equipment. *Renewal and replacement funds* account for resources held for renovation or replacement of existing facilities. *Retirement of indebtedness funds* account for resources to be used for repayment of principal and interest on long-term debt. The major assets of these funds are cash and investments.

The *investment in plant fund* consists of fixed assets, debt associated with the fixed assets, and a fund balance account, Net Investment in Plant. This is where the depreciation allowance and corresponding provision for depreciation may be recorded pursuant to *GASB Statement 8.*

Hospitals

Government-owned hospitals are accounted for as enterprise funds of the sponsoring government. However, most hospitals adhere to similar reporting standards whether they are government-owned, private nonprofit, or for-profit. Since hospitals sell their services to individual users and generally bill most charges to third-party payors, accounting practices are similar in many ways to those of business organizations.

Hospitals use a current unrestricted or general fund (often referred to in the plural as general funds) to account for all revenues and expenses, and report these on an income statement. Accrual accounting is used, and expenses (including depreciation) rather than expenditures are recorded. Other funds record additions and deductions on a statement of changes in fund balances.

Unlike most other nonprofit organizations, hospitals record fixed assets and long-term liabilities in the current unrestricted or general fund. In most respects, the transactions recorded in this fund are like those of business organizations. Board-designated assets are included in the current unrestricted or general fund as the governing board is free to remove the designation at any time.

Hospital-restricted funds include specific-purpose funds, endowment funds, and plant replacement and expansion funds. Donor-restricted resources for general operating purposes are accounted for as "other operating revenue" or "deferred revenue" in the restricted–specific-purpose or current restricted funds. Hospital endowment funds are similar to those of colleges and universities including endowments and term endowments. Endowment resources that become available for unrestricted purposes should be shown as nonoperating revenue. In general, resources provided for a specific operating activity are accounted for within the current restricted fund and resources provided for other restricted purposes such as acquiring land, etc., are accounted for as restricted–specific-purpose funds.

For example, assume the general fund incurs a cost of $10,000 for a purpose associated with a specific-purpose fund. The current unrestricted fund would record

Expense	10,000	
Accounts Payable		10,000
Due from Specific-Purpose Fund	10,000	
Other Operating Revenues		10,000

The special-purpose fund would record

Transfers to Current Unrestricted Fund	10,000	
Due to General Fund		10,000

Third-party reimbursement from insurers heavily dominates hospital accounting; receivables and allowance accounts are needed to reflect the insurer receivables, and allowance must be made for amounts insurers will not pay. Patient service revenue is reported at the gross amount billed and three major categories or adjustments are subtracted to arrive at net patient service revenue in the operating statement. The three adjustment categories are (1) charity allowances for the differences between amounts billed and received for indigent patients, (2) courtesy allowance or policy discounts to represent the differences between established rates and amounts received from doctors, staff, or others, and (3) contractual adjustments to represent the differences between amounts billed and paid by third-party payors such as Medicare and insurance companies. Donations and pledges are recognized as nonoperating revenue in the year for which the donor specified use and also recorded in restricted or unrestricted funds depending upon the donor's specification.

Voluntary Health and Welfare Organizations

Typical funds used by voluntary health and welfare organizations include current unrestricted and restricted funds, land, building and equipment fund, endowment funds, and custodian (agency) funds. The accrual basis should be used if possible.

Revenue accounting for voluntary health and welfare organizations is especially concerned with accounting for pledges and donations. A distinction is made between revenues, such as membership dues, and "public support." Contributions and proceeds from fund raising activities are reported as public support. Generally, pledges and donations are recognized in the fiscal period in which the donor specifies they are to be spent.

Investments for use in acquiring plant assets, as well as plant assets, and associated debt are recorded in the land, building and equipment fund. Resources restricted for endowment purposes are accounted for in endowment funds. Operating activities are accounted for in the current funds.

The financial reporting of voluntary health and welfare organizations is characterized by a junctional classification of both revenues (public support or revenue) and expenses (program services or supporting services). This functional classification is intended to permit users to determine how much of the revenues were utilized for the program the organization was created to support and solicited funds for. Public support revenues include contributions, special events, bequests, and campaigns. Revenue includes membership dues, investment income, and realized gain on investments. Program service expenses include research, and all expenses associated with the organizations' primary programs. Supporting services include all administrative expenses including management and fund raising.

Typical transactions of voluntary health and welfare organizations include

1 As a result of a campaign to raise funds, an organization receives the following gifts and pledges:

```
Unrestricted cash donations................................... $ 25,000
Unrestricted pledges............................................  300,000
Restricted cash donations ...................................   10,000
Restricted pledges..............................................   80,000
```

Five percent of the pledges are estimated to be uncollectible. The following journal entries would be made:

CURRENT UNRESTRICTED FUND

```
Cash ................................................  25,000
Pledges Receivable...................................  300,000
    Allowance for Uncollectible Pledges ....................   15,000
    Support—Contributions ..................................  310,000
```

CURRENT RESTRICTED FUND

```
Cash .....................................................  10,000
Pledges Receivable...................................  80,000
    Allowance for Uncollectible Pledges ......................   4,000
    Support—Contributions ....................................  86,000
```

2 Unrestricted pledges of $287,000 and restricted pledges of $75,000 are received. The remainder of the outstanding pledges are written off:

CURRENT UNRESTRICTED FUND

```
Cash .................................................  287,000
Allowance for Uncollectible Pledges...............   13,000
    Pledges Receivable ......................................  300,000
```

CURRENT RESTRICTED FUND

```
Cash .................................................  75,000
Allowance for Uncollectible Pledges.................   5,000
    Pledges Receivable ......................................   80,000
```

Other transactions recorded in the current unrestricted fund include:

3 Membership fees of $50,000 are received:

```
Cash ....................................................  50,000
    Revenues—Membership Fees ............................  50,000
```

4 Services are donated to the organizations with a value of $20,000:

```
Expenses...............................................  20,000
    Support—Donated Services...............................  20,000
```

5 Operating expenses of $220,000 are incurred; $200,000 of which have been paid:

Expenses... 220,000	
Cash..	200,000
Accounts Payable	20,000

Typical transactions of the land, buildings and equipment fund would include:

1 A grant of $100,000 for the purchase of equipment was received:

Cash 100,000	
Support—Contributions	100,000

2 Equipment is purchased for $98,000:

Equipment.. 98,000	
Cash..	98,000

3 Depreciation of $16,000 is recorded on the equipment for the fiscal period:

Depreciation Expense 16,000	
Accumulated Depreciation................................	16,000

Other Nonprofit Organizations

Accounting for other nonprofit organizations is similar in most respects to accounting for voluntary health and welfare organizations. Some fund titles differ between the two types of organizations. The current funds used by voluntary health and welfare organizations are sometimes called operating fund—unrestricted and operating fund—restricted by other nonprofit organizations. The land, building, and equipment fund is often called the plant fund.

Restricted support is recognized as revenue by other nonprofit organizations only at the time an expenditure is made from these resources that qualifies under the terms of the restriction. This support would be recorded as a liability (deferred support) until expenditures are made. Voluntary health and welfare organizations recognize these resources as revenue when received.

SUMMARY

This chapter described several complex transactions that occur in governmental and nonprofit organizations. Many more transactions occur which have not been described. GASB statements provide guidance for complex investment transactions not discussed in this book. The objective of this book has been to convey a basic understanding of nonprofit organization accounting and financial reporting. More comprehensive texts are available for those who have a need to expand their understanding beyond the basics.

KEY CONCEPTS AND TERMS

Ad valorem
Property tax assessment
Tax levy
Allowance for uncollectible taxes
Taxes receivable—current
Taxes receivable—delinquent
Allowance for uncollectible delinquent taxes
Interest and penalties receivable—taxes
Allowance for uncollectible interest and penalties
Deferred revenues
Tax liens receivable
Allowance for uncollectible tax liens
Contracts payable
Contracts payable—retained percentage

Construction-in-progress
Investment in general fixed assets
Operating revenues
Nonoperating revenues
Revenue bonds
Unreserved retained earnings
Expendable trust
Nonexpendable trust
Additions and deductions
Mandatory and nonmandatory transfers
Loan funds
Current funds
Endowment funds
Plant funds
Specific-purpose funds
Custodian funds

DISCUSSION QUESTIONS

1 What is the purpose of a tax levy? How is a tax levy related to a tax assessment?

2 When are property taxes considered to be realized by governmental units? Why?

3 List the primary steps of the property tax collection cycle. How does this cycle relate to a governmental unit's fiscal year?

4 How is the estimate of uncollectible taxes treated by a governmental unit? How does this treatment differ from the treatment of estimated bad debts by business organizations?

5 At what time and why are property taxes reclassified as being delinquent?

6 What does a lien represent? Why is it important in accounting for property taxes?

7 List the steps in the capital projects cycle.

8 How is the authorization to spend money for construction recorded in a capital projects fund?

9 How are the awarding of a contract and amounts for construction billed to the government recorded in a capital projects fund?

10 How is the amount of construction-in-progress accounted for at fiscal year-end?

11 What happens to a capital projects fund when the construction financed by the fund is completed?

12 What is a special assessment? What funds are used to account for such an activity?

13 How and why is the accounting for proprietary funds similar to accounting for business organizations?

14 What kinds of services normally are provided through proprietary funds? Why?

15 How is revenue recognition different between proprietary and fiduciary funds?

16 How are revenue bonds different from general obligation bonds? How does this difference affect the accounting for the bonds?

17 How does accounting for depreciation differ between proprietary and governmental fund assets? Why?

18 How do expendable trust funds differ from nonexpendable trust funds? How do these differences affect accounting for the funds?

19 What are the unique attributes of agency funds that affect accounting for these funds?

20 What basis of accounting do most nonprofit organizations use? Why?

21 What funds are used to account for the major operating activities of nonprofit organizations?

22 Which university and hospital funds recognize revenues and expenditures? Why is this recognition limited to these funds?

23 The current restricted funds of colleges and universities recognize revenue only in an amount equal to expenditures. Why?

24 What accounting treatment is provided for the earnings of endowment funds of nonprofit organizations such as colleges and universities?

25 What are the primary categories of plant funds used by colleges and universities? Compare the plant funds to the funds and account groups used by governmental organizations.

26 How is accounting for operating activities of hospitals different from that of governmental organizations? How are the general funds of these types of organizations different?

27 What is the purpose of hospital plant replacement and expansion funds?

28 What is unique about the revenue and expense accounting of voluntary health and welfare organizations?

29 What is the purpose of land, buildings, and equipment funds of voluntary health and welfare organizations?

PROBLEMS

1 The following events relate to the property tax levy and collection of taxes by the City of Smith Junction:

   a Property taxes of $3,200,000 were levied on March 1, 19X1. Taxes are due by May 1, Three percent of the taxes are estimated to be uncollectible. Smith Junction's fiscal year ends June 30. The accountant estimates that 8 percent of the taxes will be collected after August 1, 19X1, and, therefore, will not be available for current year expenditures.

   b By May 1, 19X1, 75 percent of the taxes had been collected. On that date, the remaining unpaid taxes were reclassified as delinquent along with the allowance for uncollectible taxes.

c   By June 30, 19X1, all but 12 percent of the taxes had been collected along with $36,000 of interest and penalties. An additional $7,000 of interest and penalties had accrued on delinquent taxes. Liens were issued for the unpaid taxes and the allowance for uncollectible taxes was closed.

d   On July 1, 19X1, the deferred revenues were reclassified.

e   By September 1, 19X1, all but 2 percent of the property taxes and $1,000 of related interest and penalties had been collected. The remaining taxes were written off as uncollectible.

Required:
Provide the journal entries necessary to record the transactions associated with these events in Smith Junction's general fund.

2   The following events relate to the County of Bent Brook:

a   On May 1, 19X1, the County Board of Commissioners authorized the expenditure of $4,000,000 for the construction of a new county building. Half of the amount will be provided from a federal grant and half will be financed by issuing bonds.

b   On June 1, 19X1, the general obligation bonds were issued at face value and a receivable was recorded for the grant.

c   On July 1, 19X1, a contract was awarded for $4,000,000 for the construction project. The federal grant was received.

d   By September 30, 19X1, the end of the County's fiscal year, $1,200,000 of cost on the project had been submitted to the County for payment. This amount was paid net of the retained percentage. The contract provided for a retained percentage of 10 percent until final completion and approval of the building.

e   By May 1, 19X2, the construction had been completed. The total cost of the construction was $3,850,000. The contractor was paid the amount due less the retained percentage.

f   On May 20, 19X2, the building was approved and final payments were made to the contractor. Remaining cash was transferred to the debt service fund.

Required:
Provide all the journal entries necessary to record these events in the appropriate funds and account groups of the County of Bent Brook.

3   The City of Old Tree operates a water utility as an enterprise fund. The following events relate to the operations of the fund for the month of November:

a   Customers were billed for water consumed in the amount of $88,000. Uncollectible accounts were estimated at one-half of 1 percent of the amount billed to customers. The City general fund was billed for $300.

b   The utility incurred $54,000 in operating costs and $10,000 in depreciation expense on equipment.

c   Revenue bonds in the amount of $400,000 were issued for the purchase of equipment.

d   Equipment was purchased for $170,000 during the month.

e   Interest accrued on the bonds was $2,000 by the end of the month.

Required:

Prepare the journal entries necessary to record these events in the water utility fund for the month. Prepare a statement of revenues, expenses, and changes in retained earnings for the fund for November. Retained earnings on November 1 were $8,000.

4 The Village of Silver Forge maintains a garage to service its vehicles. The garage is accounted for as an internal service fund. At the beginning of 19X1, the following balances existed in the accounts of the garage fund:

	Debit	Credit
Cash	$ 800	
Due from General Fund	3,000	
Supplies	6,500	
Machinery and Equipment	42,000	
Allowance for Depreciation—Machinery and Equipment		$ 16,000
Buildings	75,000	
Allowance for Depreciation—Buildings		24,000
Land	4,500	
Due to Utility Fund		120
Accounts Payable		1,400
Advance from General Fund		70,000
Retained Earnings		20,280
	$131,800	$131,800

The following transactions occurred during 19X1:

a Charges to other funds for the year were

General fund	$58,000
Special revenue fund	12,000

b Cash received from charges:

General fund	$59,500
Special revenue fund	11,800

c Paid salaries and wages of $32,000. Accrued salaries and wages at year-end amounted to $500.

d Utility bills received during the year amounted to $3,400. The unpaid balance at year-end was $350.

e Supplies purchased on account during the year amounted to $18,000. The amount of supplies on hand at year-end was $2,600.

f Operating expenses paid for the year were $8,400.

g The balance in Accounts Payable at year-end was $750.

h Depreciation on the machinery and equipment amounted to $4,800. Depreciation on the building was $5,000.

i The $70,000 advance from the general fund is received.

Required:

a Journalize all the entries necessary to account for the operations of the garage fund for 19X1. Include adjusting and closing entries.

b Prepare a statement of revenues, expenses, and changes in retained earnings and a balance sheet for the garage fund for 19X1.

5 On February 1, 19X1, the City of Green Shores received a gift of property and securities as an endowment for the support of a public library. The endowment will be accounted for in a nonexpendable trust fund, the library endowment fund. Earnings from the endowment will be used to purchase books and periodicals for the library and will be accounted for in an expendable trust fund, the library support fund. The endowment consists of $750,000 of rental property at fair market value and $750,000 of securities at face and market value. The following events occurred during 19X1:

a The rental property was leased for $80,000 for the remainder of the year. This amount was received in monthly installments and was fully paid by year-end.

b Depreciation on the rental property for the year was $8,000.

c Management and maintenance fees for the property amounted to $3,000.

d Interest and dividends of $16,000 were received. An additional $4,000 of interest has accrued on the securities by year-end.

e Cash of $75,000 was transferred from the nonexpendable to the expendable trust fund.

f Books and periodicals amounting to $72,000 were purchased during the year. Of this amount, $2,000 remains unpaid at year-end.

Required:

a Prepare the journal entries in the nonexpendable and expendable trust funds to record these transactions, including adjusting and closing entries.

b Prepare a statement of revenues, expenses (or expenditures), and changes in fund balance and a balance sheet for the nonexpendable and expendable trust funds for 19X1.

6 The County of Red Clay maintains an agency fund to collect property taxes for two incorporated towns, Hill and Dale, and for the county school district. The taxes are shared as follows:

County of Red Clay	20 percent
County school district	40 percent
Town of Hill	30 percent
Town of Dale	10 percent

On February 1, 19X1, $800,000 of property taxes were levied. By March 30, 19X1, $600,000 of the taxes had been collected.

Required:

Record these events in the County of Red Clay agency fund.

7 The current funds balance sheet for Red Rock College for the fiscal year ended August 31, 19X1, is presented below:

Red Rock College
Current Funds Balance Sheet
August 31, 19X1

Assets

Unrestricted:

Cash..	$140,000
Accounts receivable—net of allowance for uncollectible accounts of $7,500..	270,000
Prepaid expenses...	28,000
Total unrestricted...	$438,000

Restricted:

Cash..	$ 9,000
Investments...	150,000
Total restricted..	$159,000
Total current funds	$597,000

Liabilities and Fund Balances

Unrestricted:

Accounts payable...	$ 87,000
Due to student loan fund	32,000
Fund balance..	319,000
Total unrestricted...	$438,000

Restricted:

Due to unrestricted funds..	$ 12,000
Fund balance..	147,000
Total restricted..	$159,000
Total current funds	$597,000

The following event occurred during 19X2:

a Student tuition and fees amounted to $2,350,000. Two percent of this amount was estimated as uncollectible. Accounts receivable of $10,000 were written off as uncollectible during the year. The balance in Accounts Receivable at year-end was $189,000.

b A state appropriation of $1,900,000 was recorded. Of this amount, $250,000 had not been received by year-end. The appropriation was unrestricted.

c Cash donations of $200,000 were received. Of this amount $80,000 was restricted for scholarships. The remainder was unrestricted.

d Investment income of $12,000 was earned and received. Investment income is transferred to the unrestricted fund. The balance due the unrestricted fund at year-end was $9,000.

e Unrestricted operating expenses of $3,460,000 were incurred. The balance in Accounts Payable at year-end was $75,000

f The unrestricted fund transferred $60,000 to the plant retirement of indebtedness fund and $75,000 to the student loan fund. An additional $4,000 was owed the student loan fund at year-end.

Required:
Provide journal entries for each transaction for the current funds.

8 The following events occurred for Plains City Hospital during 19X1:

a Nursing services revenue was $850,000. Other professional services revenue was $450,000. All revenue is charged on account. Of these revenues, $60,000 are estimated to be uncollectible.

b Unrestricted contributions of $75,000 were made to the operating fund. Earnings received on endowment fund investments amounted to $55,000.

c The beginning balance in Accounts Receivable was $90,000. The ending balance was $105,000. Accounts for $52,000 were written off as uncollectible.

d Costs incurred and paid during the year included:

Administrative expenses	$286,000
Nursing service expenses	710,000
Other professional services expenses	320,000
Supplies purchased	112,000

e Supplies used during the year amounted to $106,000.

f A federal grant of $225,000 restricted for the purchase of equipment was received and equipment was purchased for this amount.

g Depreciation of $80,000 was recorded on buildings and $110,000 was recorded on equipment.

h Investment income of $45,000 was earned and received by the plant renewal and replacement fund. An additional $8,000 in revenue was accrued at year-end.

Required:
Provide the journal entries needed to record each transaction and indicate the fund in which the entry would be recorded.

Index

Account group:
    fixed assets, 12, 34, 117–119, 138–139
    long-term debt, 13, 34, 119–122, 139
Accounting standards, 17
Accrual basis, 14, 37–38
Advances (*see* Transfers)
AICPA, 17–20
Appropriations, 103–106, 113–115
Assessment (*see* Property taxes)
Assets:
    current, 12
    definition of, 11
    fixed, 12, 117–119
Audit guides, 19–20, 96
Auditing, 19, 83, 94–95
Auxiliary enterprises, 15, 150

Balance sheet:
    governmental, 41–45
    nonprofit, 45–48
Bond ratings, 75, 81
Bonds:
    general obligation, 74, 77–80, 120
    revenue, 74–77, 120, 142–143
budget cycle, 102–103
budgetary accounting, 103–107, 116–117,
    136–139
Budgetary control, 14–15, 29, 58–60,
    86

Capital maintenance, 2, 9, 32, 119
Cash flows, 60–61, 75
Closing entries, 116–117, 133, 136–137,
    143
Colleges and universities, 149–153
Combined financial statements, 40, 53
Combining financial statements, 40, 53
Competitive market, 2, 5

Compliance audit, 83, 94–96
Comprehensive annual financial report,
    30
Constituents, 87–90
Construction in progress, 44, 136–138
Control, accounting, 28
Creditors, 30, 73–83

Debt service, 75–79
Default risk, 74
Delinquent taxes, 131–133
Depreciation, 10, 56–57, 119, 143
Disclosure, 62–63, 86
Donations, 16, 154

Encumbrances, 53, 113–115, 135–138
Entity, 13
Expenditures, 9, 28, 52, 79, 113–115,
    135–137
Expenses, 9, 56, 142

Financial Accounting Standards Board,
    17–20
Financial audit, 94–96
Financial position (*see* Balance sheet)
Financial ratios, 75, 82, 86
Financial reporting:
    objectives, 27–30, 64–65
    pyramid, 39
    user information needs, 29–30
Financial resources, 9, 37–38
Free riders, 3
Fund:
    agency, 33, 145–146
    annuity and life income, 48
    capital projects, 32, 133–139
    control, 28

Fund (*Cont.*):
  current restricted, 150–152, 154–156
  current unrestricted, 35, 150–156
  custodial, 35
  debt service, 32
  definition of, 31
  endowment, 35, 48, 151–153
  enterprise, 32, 140–143, 153
  expendable trust, 33
  fiduciary, 33, 143–146
  general, 31, 153
  governmental, 31
  internal service, 32, 140–143
  loan, 35
  nonexpendable trust, 33
  nonprofit, 35, 147–149
  pension trust, 33
  plant, 35, 48, 152–153
  proprietary, 32, 140–143
  restricted, 35
  special revenue, 32, 113
  specific purpose, 48, 153
  trust, 33, 144–145
Fund balance:
  changes in, 56
  definition of, 44–45
  reserved, 117
  unreserved, 103, 116–117
Fungible resources, 12

General-purpose financial statements, 30, 53
Going concern, 10
Goods and services:
  jointly consumed, 7
  public, 3
  separable, 3, 6, 32
Governmental accounting concepts, 8–15
Governmental Accounting Standards Board, 17–20
Governmental auditing standards, 95
Governmental Finance Officers Association, 19
Governmental organization attributes, 7
Grants, 30, 83–85, 135–136, 142, 151

Hospitals, 153–154

Income statement (*see* Operating results)
Interfund transactions (*see* Transfers)
Intergenerational equity, 11, 39, 52, 74

Intergovernmental revenues, 112–113
Investments, 109

Leases, 122
Legal control, 15
Legal environment, 5, 17
Liabilities:
  current, 12
  definition of, 12
  long-term, 12, 80, 119–122, 134–136
Liquidity, 77

Market risk, 81
Matching concept, 9–10, 14
Measurement focus, 37
Modified accrual basis, 14, 37

National Council on Governmental Accounting, 17–20
Nonprofit accounting principles, 15–16
Nonprofit organizations:
  definition of, 2
  goals, 3
  types of, 15–16

Operating results:
  for governments, 49–54
  for nonprofit organizations, 54
Operating transfers (*see* Transfers)
Other financing sources and uses, 52, 104
Other nonprofit organizations, 156
Overlapping debt, 78
Oversight groups, 2, 30, 85–87

Performance audit, 94–95
Pledges, 154
Political environment, 5, 17
Profit, 5, 9
Property taxes, 128–133
Public policy, 2, 5
Public schools, 149

Quasi-external transactions, 112

Rate of return, 74
Reserve for supplies, 117

Reserve funds, 77
Residual equity transfers, 109
Return on investment, 2, 5
Revenue stability, 76
Revenues, 8, 49, 74, 107–108, 128–133,
    141–142
  estimated, 104–106

Securities and Exchange Commission, 17
Single audit, 19, 84, 95–96
Sinking funds (*see* Reserve funds)
Special assessments, 139–140
Special interest groups, 89
Subsidiary accounts, 106

Tax base, 78–79
Tax levy, 128–133, 139
Tax liens, 132–133
Tax rates, 78
Taxes (*see* Revenues; Property taxes)
Third-party payments, 15, 83–84,
    153
Transfers, 52–54, 104, 109–112, 153

Uncollectable taxes, 130–133

Voluntary Health and Welfare
    Organizations, 154–156